The Darkness and the DAWN

BIBLE STUDY GUIDE

From the Bible-teaching ministry of

CHARLES R. SWINDOLL

INSIGHT FOR LIVING

Insight for Living's Bible teacher, Chuck Swindoll, has devoted his life to the clear, practical application of God's Word and His grace. A pastor at heart, Chuck has served as senior pastor to congregations in Texas, Massachusetts, and California. He currently leads Stonebriar Community Church in Frisco, Texas, but Chuck's listening audience extends far beyond a local church body. As a leading program in Christian broadcasting, *Insight for Living* airs in major Christian radio markets, through more than 2,100 outlets worldwide, in 16 languages, and to a growing webcast audience. Chuck's extensive writing ministry has also served the body of Christ worldwide, and his leadership as president and now chancellor of Dallas Theological Seminary has helped prepare and equip a new generation for ministry. Chuck and Cynthia, his partner in life and ministry, have four grown children and ten grandchildren.

Based on the outlines, charts, and transcripts of Charles R. Swindoll's sermons, the Bible study guide text was developed and written by the Pastoral Ministries Department of Insight for Living.

Editor in Chief:
Cynthia Swindoll

Study Guide Writer:
Mark Tobey

Senior Editor and Assistant Writer:
Wendy Peterson

Editor and Assistant Writer:
Marla DeShong

Editor:
Amy LaFuria

Rights and Permissions:
The Meredith Agency

Text Designer:
Gary Lett

Typesetter:
Bob Haskins

Unless otherwise identified, all Scripture references are from the New American Standard Bible, © The Lockman Foundation 1960, 1962, 1963, 1968, 1971, 1972, 1973, 1975, 1977, 1995. Used by permission. Scripture taken from the Holy Bible, New International Version, Copyright © 1973, 1978, 1984 International Bible Society, used by permission of Zondervan Bible Publishers [NIV]. Scripture quotations from THE MESSAGE © 1993, 1994, 1995 by Eugene H. Peterson. Used by permission of NavPress Publishing Group.

Copyright © 2002 by Insight for Living

Fourteen of the chapters in this study guide first appeared as outlines of Chuck's sermons in the series titled *Christ's Agony and Ecstasy* that were edited and expanded by Ed Neuenschwander with the assistance of Bill Butterworth:

Copyright © 1982 by Charles R. Swindoll

Original outlines, charts, and transcripts:

Copyright © 1972, 1973, 1974, 1975, 1976, 1980, 1984, 1991, 1992, 1993, 2000 by Charles R. Swindoll, Inc.

An effort has been made to locate sources and obtain permission where necessary for the quotations used in this book. In the event of any unintentional omission, a modification will gladly be incorporated in future printings.

ISBN 1-57972-390-X
Cover design: Adapted from the hardback cover design by Uttley/DouPonce DesignWorks
Cover image: © 2001 William J. Hebert/Stone
Printed in the United States of America

CONTENTS

THE DARKNESS
Part One

A NOTE TO THE READER

This study guide was written to correspond with *The Darkness and the Dawn* cassette series and serves as an excellent ancillary study to Chuck's book *The Darkness and the Dawn: Empowered by the Triumph and Tragedy of the Cross* (Nashville, Tenn.: Word Publishing Company, 2001). The study guide chapters correspond with the chapter titles in the book, with a couple of exceptions. The study guide chapter titled "The Way of the Cross," chapter 7, actually appears in the book as two chapters: "The Way of the Cross," chapter 7, and "The Darkest of All Days," chapter 8. The study guide chapter titled "The Day God Answered, 'Amen,'" chapter 16, does not appear in the book.

We hope the cassette series and the Bible study guide will bring added depth and insight to your study of the death and resurrection of Jesus Christ. We believe these resources, along with Chuck's book, *The Darkness and the Dawn*, will maximize your understanding of this monumental topic, and deepen your relationship with the living Savior!

Insight for Living

INTRODUCTION

Jesus' death on the cross for the sins of humanity marked the darkest time in the history of the world. Journey with me back in time to this landmark event and explore the circumstances surrounding the crucifixion of our suffering Savior. There, you will gain new insights into His deity, His character, His work, and especially His infinite love for His creation.

As you view the darkness and the dawn together, you will see that Christ's love led Him to an excruciating death on the cross. But the story doesn't end there. His decisive victory over death was profoundly illustrated by the empty tomb.

Let's return now to the darkness of His Passion and on into the glorious dawn of His resurrection. Experience the triumph, hope, and victory over sin and death that He purchased for you and for me on the cross. You'll be deeply moved by the overflowing tragedy and then greatly encouraged by the glorious triumph of the greatest story of all time—the story of the cruel cross and the empty tomb.

Chuck Swindoll

Charles R. Swindoll

PUTTING TRUTH
INTO ACTION

K nowledge apart from application falls short of God's desire for
His children. He wants us to apply what we learn so that we
will change and grow. This Bible study guide was prepared with
these goals in mind. As you go through the following pages, we
hope your desire to discover biblical truth will grow as your understanding of God's Word increases and that you will be encouraged
to apply what you've learned.

To assist you in your study, we've included a section called
Living Insights at the end of each lesson. These exercises will
challenge you to study further and to think of specific ways to put
your discoveries into action.

On occasion a lesson is followed by a Digging Deeper section, which gives you additional information and resources to probe
further into issues raised in that lesson.

There are many ways to use this guide—in personal devotions,
group studies, discussions with friends and family, and Sunday School
classes. And, of course, it's an ideal study aid when you're listening
to its corresponding *Insight for Living* radio series.

To benefit most from this Bible study guide, we encourage you
to consider it a spiritual journal. That's why we've included space
in the **Living Insights** for recording your thoughts and discoveries.
We hope you'll return to those sections often for review and en-
couragement as you continue to grow in your walk with Christ.

Insight for Living

The Darkness and the DAWN

THE DARKNESS

When the sixth hour had come, darkness fell over the whole land . . . (Mark 15:33)

On the day that Christ died, a shadow fell like sackcloth across the land. It was as if creation were mourning the death of its Maker. The light of the sky dimmed as the Light of the world was snuffed out.

Darkness and death culminated the final period of Jesus' life known as the Passion—"the sufferings of Christ between the night of the Last Supper and His death."[1] It lasted just a few hours, really. Not even a full day. Yet, as theologian Richard John Neuhaus expressed, the Passion is humanity's epochal event:

> Every human life, conceived from eternity and destined to eternity, here finds its story truly told. In this killing that some call senseless we are brought to our senses. Here we find out who we most truly are, because here is the One who is what we are called to be. [Jesus] cries, "Come, follow me." Follow Him there? We recoil. We close our ears. We hurry on to Easter. But we will not know what to do with Easter's light if we shun the friendship of the darkness that is wisdom's way to light.[2]

In the darkness of Christ's Passion, the blackness of humanity's sin and the power of divine love clash—and love wins! Through Christ's suffering, our sins are atoned. "I have been crucified with Christ," Paul exclaims (Gal. 2:20a). Christ's death is our death, and in that death, we find eternal life.

We invite you to linger through the Passion of our Lord. Pause often, watch quietly, and take heart. This is your story.

---

1. *Webster's Ninth New Collegiate Dictionary*, see "passion."

2. Richard John Neuhaus, *Death on a Friday Afternoon: Meditations on the Last Words of Jesus from the Cross* (New York, N.Y.: Perseus Books Group, Basic Books, 2000), p. 2.

Chapter 1

THE SUFFERING SAVIOR

Isaiah 52:13–53:12

Centuries ago on the south coast of China, high on a hill overlooking the harbor of Macao, Portuguese settlers built an enormous cathedral. They believed it would weather time, so they placed as its centerpiece a massive bronze cross that reached high into the sky. Not too many years later, a typhoon came. God's fingerwork swept away man's handiwork, and every stone of the magnificent cathedral crumbled down the hill into the ocean as debris. All that remained unmoved by the storm's fury were fragments of the front wall and the cross.

Centuries later a shipwreck stranded hundreds of men not far out in that same harbor. Some died. A few lived. One of the men left hanging onto wreckage from the ship was disoriented and frightened, having lost sight of land. Yet, each time the ocean's swells lifted him out of the waves, he spotted the cross, which eventually guided him to safety.

To countless millions, that is what the cross means. It's a glowing symbol of rescue, leading stranded souls, shipwrecked on sin's jagged reefs, from the shadow of death's darkness to the shining shores of new life dawned. But it is also a place of hope to countless Christians who come *back* to the cross, bringing the scattered debris of their lives—lives buffeted by the blows of an extramarital affair or the ruinous consequences of a sinful addiction, others broken in two by the heartrending loss of a lifelong mate or the tormenting shame of abuse. All are invited to the cross, to the place where God and humanity meet, where peace and wholeness can be found.

Soul-rescuing power, however, doesn't rest in the symbol of the cross, but in the One who bore its shame. So the invitation is not to a place, but to a Person. To the One whose violent suffering and crushing death wrought a wondrous, *saving* work—a springtide of mercy and grace to the world.

It is to Him and His work that we turn in this study.

We'll first encounter Him in Isaiah 52 and 53. Centuries prior to Christ's Passion, the prophet Isaiah wrote in amazing detail of Jesus' suffering, His shameful rejection by His own, and His redeeming death. It's important that we pause here to linger . . . to sense the pain . . . to observe the reproach . . . to marvel at the cost . . . to explore the wonder of how that which "was separated by an abyss of wrong, was reconciled by the deed of perfect love."[1]

His Mission

Isaiah 52:13–53:12 is one of four "servant songs" in Isaiah that prophesy the Messiah—called here, God's Servant—the Savior who rescues us from sin's death-grip and gives us new, blessed life. (The other songs are in 42:1–9; 49:1–13; 50:4–11.) Each of the five stanzas in this song throbs with the Servant's pain—pain that encompasses all the world's wounds . . . and all its ability to wound.

> Behold, My servant will prosper,
> He will be high and lifted up and greatly exalted.
> Just as many were astonished at you, My people,
> So His appearance was marred more than any man
> And His form more than the sons of men.
> Thus He will sprinkle many nations,
> Kings will shut their mouths on account of Him;
> For what had not been told them they will see,
> And what they had not heard they will understand.
> (Isa. 52:13–15)

The Servant whom God will greatly honor will have a glory likened to God's own glory—He will "be high and lifted up," just as the Lord is "lofty and exalted" (compare 6:1).[2]

Before He is glorified, however, the Servant will suffer. He will be "marred," His face and body disfigured. What an accurate picture of Jesus Isaiah gives us. Many centuries later, Jesus' face and body

---

1. Richard John Neuhaus, *Death on a Friday Afternoon: Meditations on the Last Words of Jesus from the Cross* (New York, N.Y.: Basic Books, 2000), p. 34.

2. The Hebrew words are identical in Isaiah 6:1 and 52:13: the words *lofty* and *high* are both *rum* in Hebrew, and *exalted* and *lifted up* are both *nasa* in Hebrew.

were marred from beatings He received at the hands of the Sanhedrin (Matt. 26:67; Mark 14:65), from the scourging and abuse of the Roman soldiers (Matt. 27:26–31; Mark 15:15–19; John 19:1–3), and from the six hours of agony hanging on the cross (Matt. 27:33–46; Mark 15:22–37; Luke 23:33–46; John 19:16–34).

Isaiah writes that, through His death, the Servant "will sprinkle many nations," meaning that He will cleanse many people, Jews and Gentiles, of their sin (see Heb. 9:26b–10:22). Isaiah prophesied that the One "whom many have not considered important at all, will actually provide the most important thing."[3] When the world in all its self-exalting conceit realizes that, its only response will be a stunned, grieved silence (see Rev. 1:7).

His Rejection

In the second stanza, Isaiah explores more deeply the Servant's rejection. One would think that people would eagerly welcome God's Good News, but they never have. When Isaiah wrote of God's Servant, he was proclaiming a gospel of deliverance (Isa. 53:1), and he fully expected a response of faith. Sadly, the opening verses of Isaiah 53 reveal little faith among God's people:

> Who has believed our message?
> And to whom has the arm of the Lord been revealed?
> For He grew up before Him like a tender shoot,
> And like a root out of parched ground;
> He has no stately form or majesty
> That we should look upon Him,
> Nor appearance that we should be attracted to Him.
> He was despised and forsaken of men,
> A man of sorrows acquainted with grief;
> And like one from whom men hide their face
> He was despised, and we did not esteem Him.
> (vv. 1–3)

Israel expected a mighty, valiant conqueror to storm her enemies' gates and lead her to freedom in a blaze of victory. Instead, the "arm of the Lord" stretched out through a different kind of Deliverer, Jesus Christ, who in the eyes of the people, didn't fit the mold.

3. John A. Martin, "Isaiah," in *The Bible Knowledge Commentary*, Old Testament edition, ed. John F. Walvoord and Roy B. Zuck (Colorado Springs, Colo.: Chariot Victor Publishing, 1985), p. 1107.

First of all, Jesus' pedigree was unimpressive (v. 2). From His childhood ("tender root"), there was nothing that distinguished Him from run-of-the-mill kind of folk. In fact, He came from less than most others—"parched ground"—and resembled an inconsequential weed, struggling for life in the barrenness of Judah.

Second, His physical appearance left much to be desired. He had "no stately form or majesty," no handsome-prince good looks and charisma that drew all eyes to Him. Rather, He "was a rejected person, not valued, perhaps ostracized . . . of whom nothing was expected. This is not, and never was, one of the great ones of the earth. This is one of the little ones, surely of no consequence."[4] A lonely man, well acquainted with heartbreak and pain, He was counted as nothing; people didn't give Him a thought.

His Atonement

How wrong people were about God's Son—and themselves:

> Surely *our* griefs He Himself bore,
> And *our* sorrows He carried;
> Yet we ourselves esteemed Him stricken,
> Smitten of God, and afflicted.
> But He was pierced through for *our* transgressions,
> He was crushed for *our* iniquities;
> The chastening for *our* well-being fell upon Him,
> And by His scourging *we* are healed.
> *All of us* like sheep have gone astray,
> *Each of us* has turned to his own way;
> But the Lord has caused the iniquity of *us all*
> To fall on Him. (Isa. 53:4–6, emphasis added)

They thought something was wrong with Him—that He had done something to deserve God's judgment. But it's the other way around. He carried *our* "griefs" and *our* "sorrows," literally, our spiritual sickness and pain brought on by *our* sin (v. 4a). And He suffered terribly on our behalf.

Verse 5 communicates the horror of crucifixion. He was "pierced through" and "crushed"—He endured a brutal death on a cross. The parallel phrases "for our transgressions" and "for our iniquities"

---

4. Walter Brueggemann, *Isaiah 40–66*, Westminster Bible Companion Series (Louisville, Ky.: Westminster John Knox Press, 1998), p. 145.

speak plainly of Jesus Christ's atoning work. He became our substitute, taking our place; His physical suffering made our spiritual healing possible (v. 5b).

Is anyone the exception to this rule? Not according to the prophet. "*All* of us . . . *each* of us," in all time and in every place, have wandered from our Shepherd God. As Walter Brueggemann observes:

> "We" have all been wayward, all recalcitrant, like mindless, unresponsive sheep who graze off the path without heeding the summoning voice of the shepherd; in such autonomy we wander off into jeopardy and risk. The servant has been made to answer for such waywardness.[5]

This One who we thought was of no use to anyone has become everything to all. The One rejected must now be reckoned with by sheer virtue of what He has done.

His Submission

Still, there is more to this marvelous redemption. Jesus not only took on the sins of all the undeserving, but He did so without protest or defense:

> He was oppressed and He was afflicted,
> Yet He did not open His mouth;
> Like a lamb that is led to slaughter,
> And like a sheep that is silent before its shearers,
> So He did not open His mouth.
> By oppression and judgment He was taken away;
> And as for His generation, who considered
> That He was cut off out of the land of the living
> For the transgression of my people, to whom the
> stroke was due?
> His grave was assigned with wicked men,
> Yet He was with a rich man in His death,
> Because He had done no violence,
> Nor was there any deceit in His mouth. (Isa. 53:7–9)

5. Brueggemann, *Isaiah 40–66*, p. 146.

Despite His undeserved, unjust suffering, Jesus made no verbal defense. He kept silent, "like a lamb that is led to slaughter" and "like a sheep that is silent before its shearers" (v.7). Brueggemann notes:

> This silent, vulnerable sheep absorbs the deathly blows of hostility and—in derivative Christian cadence—is the lamb that was slain, "the Lamb of God who takes away the sin of the world!" (John 1:29).[6]

According to Isaiah 53:8, His was the gravest of injustices. He was taken away to die, to be "cut off out of the land of the living," to be removed from His own generation.[7] Again, Isaiah notes that all this happened to God's Servant because of *human* transgressions; this awful stroke was *our* due!

Even in death the Servant's dignity was assaulted: He was assigned a criminal's grave. Though initially assigned an unsuitable burial plot, God's Servant was ultimately placed in the tomb of a rich man. This prophecy is remarkable, since both wicked men (the Sanhedrin and Roman officials) and a rich man (Joseph of Arimathea) were intimately involved in Christ's death and burial (see Matt. 26:3–5; 27:1–4, 22–26, 41–44, 57–60).

His Exaltation

The final verses of Isaiah's servant song describe the divine perspective of God's sovereign purpose in His Son's suffering as well as vindication for this One so unjustly condemned:

> But the Lord was pleased
> To crush Him, putting Him to grief;
> If He would render Himself as a guilt offering,
> He will see His offspring,
> He will prolong His days,
> And the good pleasure of the Lord will prosper in
>   His hand.
> As a result of the anguish of His soul,

6. Brueggemann, *Isaiah 40–66*, p. 147.

7. Commentator Geoffrey W. Grogan explains that the "phrase 'cut off' strongly suggests not only a violent, premature death but also the just judgment of God (compare for example Gen. 9:11; Exod. 12:15), not simply the oppressive judgment of men." In this way, the Messiah's unjust condemnation by men satisfied God's just demand for righteousness.

He will see it and be satisfied;
By His knowledge the Righteous One,
My Servant, will justify the many,
As He will bear their iniquities.
Therefore, I will allot Him a portion with the great,
And He will divide the booty with the strong;
Because He poured out Himself to death,
And was numbered with the transgressors;
Yet He Himself bore the sin of many,
And interceded for the transgressors.
(Isa. 53:10–12)

The Lord was *pleased* to crush and grieve and make His Servant suffer? What kind of a God would do that? The kind of God who loves us so much that He would go to the greatest lengths to spare us from judgment. The God who wants to justify us and remove guilt and sin and death. That's why the Lord was pleased with Him: this Servant-Son, Jesus, shared the same desire as His Father and gave Himself completely to secure our eternal life. As Peter echoed centuries later:

> When [Jesus] received honor and glory from God
> the Father, such an utterance as this was made to
> Him by the Majestic Glory, "This is My beloved Son
> with whom I am well-pleased." (2 Pet. 1:17)

"The heart of God," J. Alec Motyer observes, "is revealed in his delight, even at such cost, in finding and providing a guilt offering" for the people He loves.[8]

And so the Servant's abject humiliation ends in His glorious exaltation. Because of Christ's selfless, humble obedience, God "intends the servant who *gave all* to now *receive all*"[9] (compare Eph. 1:10, 22; Col. 1:17–20). The "good pleasure," or delight, of the Lord—seeking and saving His lost sheep—will thrive in His capable, loving hands. And it has, and continues to do so, in the nail-scarred hands of His Son and Servant, Jesus Christ.

The closing stanza of this hymn of redemption speaks of the glorious triumph of Christ's finished work and the accomplishment

---

8. J. Alec Motyer, *The Prophecy of Isaiah: An Introduction and Commentary* (Downers Grove, Ill.: InterVarsity Press, 1993), p. 438.

9. Brueggemann, *Isaiah 40–66*, p. 148.

of God's plan for redemption. Because Christ "poured out Himself to death," He would reap the unspeakable reward of seeing limitless numbers of once helpless sinners die with Him in faith, only to be raised to walk in newness of life.

Here in Isaiah, centuries before Christ was born, we see God's wondrous plan—to provide a Savior who will lead us out of darkness and into the radiant dawn of eternal life!

 *Living Insights*

For generations, gospel music has published the glories and triumphs of the Cross. Old favorites such as "The Old Rugged Cross," "Thanks to Calvary, I'm Not the Man I Used to Be," and the beloved gospel swing "Must Jesus Bear the Cross Alone?" remind us of Christ's saving work. What is central to our faith becomes the stuff of our singing. The cross has always been and continues to be the focal point of faith for believers. Why? How could something that originally bore such reproach and shame become a symbol of glorious victory?

The apostles can answer these questions for us. Let's look over their shoulder for a few minutes to see what they wrote about the significance of the cross. Peter wrote:

> He [Christ] Himself bore our sins in His body on the cross, so that we might die to sin and live to righteousness; for by His wounds you were healed. (1 Pet. 2:24)

And Paul told us:

> For the word of the cross is foolishness to those who are perishing, but to us who are being saved it is the power of God. (1 Cor. 1:18)

The cross, in all its horror and brutality, is God's power to save sinners. It's His way of rescuing us from death and giving us new life. The world continues to think that Christianity is "foolishness." But to those of us who have believed, what Christ did on the cross is transforming our lives.

But just as Isaiah wrote in chapter 53, the issue remains: "Who has believed?" Christ's cross has no power in our lives without faith.

The "arm of the Lord" has been revealed, but as F. B. Meyer exclaims:

> The saving might of God's glorious arm may be waiting close against us; but it is inoperative unless we are united to it by faith.[10]

Do you believe that the answer to your deepest need is a Person—a Person who died on the cross for you? Do you really believe the work of salvation is finished, that there is nothing you can do to mend the torn pieces of your life, save trusting in the redeeming power of Christ and His cross?

That is a question we all must answer today . . . before we proceed any further in our study. Otherwise, the rest is foolishness.

 Questions for Group Reflection

1. How does it impact your faith to have seen Jesus' sacrificial death prophesied in such detail by the prophet Isaiah centuries before it happened? Why do you think God foretold His Servant's suffering and death?

2. What images or ideas conveyed here by Isaiah moved you the most? How do they help you understand better and feel more deeply what Jesus went through and why He did it?

3. What does the greatness of Jesus' suffering tell you about human sin? What does it tell you about His love for you?

4. What does the servant song in this passage lead you to pray about? Share your thoughts with the group. Spend some quiet time before the Lord right now, together bringing your hearts and thoughts to Him.

10. F. B. Meyer, *Christ in Isaiah* (Fort Washington, Pa.: Christian Literature Crusade, n.d.), p. 133.

Chapter 2
THE CUP OF SACRIFICE
Luke 22:7–13; Matthew 26:20, 26–31

With Isaiah's portrait of Christ's anguished atonement fresh in our minds and hearts, let's step back in time to journey with Jesus Himself on that lonely road to the cross.

His final journey began on a spring night in Jerusalem. Jesus and His disciples—including Judas, the betrayer—reclined to eat the sacred Passover meal together. For generations, faithful Jews celebrated this feast, commemorating their deliverance from Egyptian bondage. But on this night with Jesus, the symbolism of the observance would be especially poignant. For just as an "unblemished" lamb had to be slain and its blood smeared on the Hebrews' doorposts for death to "pass over" them (Ex. 12:5, 7, 13), so Jesus, the perfect Lamb of God, would be slain and His blood smeared on the wood of a cross so that death and judgment would pass over all who trust in Him.

Where They Were

During the Feast of Unleavened Bread, highlighted by Passover, Jerusalem teemed with people. Many were tourists enjoying the related festivities; countless others were Jewish pilgrims who had traveled many miles to observe the Feast within the swelling city walls. Jesus and the disciples numbered among this throng.

Before they could partake of the meal, though, necessary preparations had to be made. Luke's gospel sets the scene for this meal, Jesus' last supper on earth:

> Then came the first day of Unleavened Bread on which the Passover lamb had to be sacrificed. And Jesus sent Peter and John, saying, "Go and prepare the Passover for us, so that we may eat it." They said to Him, "Where do You want us to prepare it?" And He said to them, "When you have entered the city, a man will meet you carrying a pitcher of water; follow him into the house that he enters. And you shall say to the owner of the house, 'The Teacher says to you, "Where is the guest room in which I

10

may eat the Passover with My disciples?"' And he will show you a large, furnished upper room; prepare it there." And they left and found everything just as He had told them; and they prepared the Passover. (Luke 22:7–13)

Jesus had apparently prearranged a place for them to observe Passover together, but notice that He didn't simply give Peter and John an address. Instead, He devised a secret signal, perhaps to elude the watchful, murderous eyes of the religious leaders until the time was right (see vv. 1–2). A man would be carrying a jar of water—a chore usually carried out by a woman—and he would be the disciples' "contact."

Just as Jesus told them, Peter and John found the man who then led them upstairs to a simple, furnished room. And there they prepared the Passover, following ancient traditions that would soon find their ultimate meaning in Jesus' approaching suffering and death.

What They Did

An entire day out of the week of Unleavened Bread was set aside for Passover preparations.[1] What did the meal entail? The grocery list for dinner may have looked something like this:

✔ 1 whole lamb, unblemished—skinless and gutted

✔ 6 servings of bitter herbs, dried and tossed in a scoured bowl

✔ 3 to 4 loaves of unleavened bread

✔ 1 large bowl of fruit puree paste for dipping

By far, the lamb required the most care in preparing. Scholar Erich Kiehl provides a helpful summary of this painstaking ritual:

> In order for all the Passover lambs [approximately 10,000] to be slaughtered and roasted by sunset, the afternoon was divided into periods. Each of the three groups was assigned a specific period to go to the

---

1. According to Leviticus 23:4–8, Passover and the Unleavened Bread took place over a period of seven days. But as J. Dwight Pentecost notes, "Since the days of the Dispersion, the Jews had added an extra day at the beginning of the eight days of this festival season and called it the Day of Preparation." *The Words and Works of Jesus Christ: A Study of the Life of Christ* (Grand Rapids, Mich.: Zondervan Publishing House, 1981), p. 415.

temple area. According to the Masoretic text of Exodus 12:6, "the whole assembly of Israel shall kill [the Passover lambs] between two evenings." This meant approximately between the hours of 2:30 and 5:30 P.M. . . .

The pilgrims entered the Court of Priests from the north side. Each cut the throat of his lamb. The blood was caught in containers of precious metal, passed down the line of priests, and poured out at the altar of burnt offering. Thereby the lives of the innocent victims were given back to God. Carrying their slaughtered lambs, the pilgrims left the Court of the Priests through a gateway on the south side. Then the lambs had to be roasted. This was normally done on pomegranate sticks. When ready, the lambs were served whole, without being cut apart.[2]

The roasted lamb represented the sacrifice of the spotless lamb from which the blood was spread on the doors of Jewish believers during the Passover (see Ex. 12). The bitter herbs—a mixture of greens and various herbs—reminded the pilgrims of the stinging bitterness their ancestors endured under centuries of bondage. The unleavened bread told of the haste in which the Hebrews were to leave Egypt. And the fruit paste was a reminder of the mortar used by Hebrew slaves in making bricks for Pharaoh's harsh regime.

Every acrid bite, every bitter swallow, reminded the Jews of the bitterness of slavery—and the sacrifice made to usher in their freedom.

With the disciples having prepared everything, it was time for the Passover meal to begin . . . and a new memorial to be inaugurated.

> While they were eating, Jesus took some bread, and after a blessing, He broke it and gave it to the disciples, and said, "Take, eat; this is My body." (Matt. 26:26)

Jesus would then most likely have prayed a traditional Hebrew prayer for the bread that may have gone something like, "Praise be to you, O Lord, Sovereign of the world, who causes bread to come

2. Erich L. Kiehl, *The Passion of Our Lord* (Grand Rapids, Mich.: Baker Book House, 1990), p. 53.

forth from the earth."[3] It is unlikely that Jesus' prayer resembled the impromptu blessings present-day believers deliver prior to an evening meal.

In fact, Jesus went beyond the ancient tradition. After the blessing, He passed to His disciples the broken fragments of bread and told them, "Take, eat; this is My body." The bread was now not just a reminder of "the swiftness of God's deliverance"[4] from Egyptian bondage; it was linked definitively to Jesus, the Bread of Life, and His impending death.

Jesus had given a new significance to the Passover bread, superseding the ancient meaning with the concept that His brokenness, His death, would secure salvation for all time. Just as the Passover signified "the greatest redemptive event" of the Old Testament and looked forward to "the coming of the messianic age," so Jesus' Last Supper now signifies the "greatest redemptive event of the [New Testament]" and points "to the arrival of the kingdom in *glory* when he comes . . . and shares the messianic banquet with his followers."[5]

Through the bread ritual, Jesus announced that He would be the offering for sin, that He would "atone vicariously for the sins of the world."[6] As He gave the bread, so He would give His life on behalf of helpless sinners, hungry for life.

Then He took the cup:

> And when He had taken a cup and given thanks,
> He gave it to them, saying, "Drink from it, all of you;
> for this is My blood of the covenant, which is poured
> out for many for forgiveness of sins." (Matt. 26:27–28)

Jesus took what may have been the third cup of blessing in the traditional Passover observance and offered another prayer of thanksgiving. The wine symbolizes blood, which in the Old Testament was used to ratify a covenant; for example, God used blood to inaugurate His covenant with His people at Mount Sinai (see

3. Kiehl, *The Passion of Our Lord*, p. 61.

4. R. H. Stein, "Last Supper," in *Dictionary of Jesus and the Gospels*, ed. Joel G. Green, Scot McKnight, and I. Howard Marshall (Downers Grove, Ill.: InterVarsity Press, 1998), section 3.1.2.

5. Stein, "Last Supper," p. 6.

6. Kiehl, *The Passion of Our Lord*, p. 61.

Ex. 24:8). In the same way, Jesus alluded to a new covenant—sealed by His own blood—which He would make with those who receive Him by faith. Sins would be forgiven, as Jeremiah had foretold:

> "Behold, days are coming," declares the Lord, "when I will make a new covenant with the house of Israel and with the house of Judah, not like the covenant which I made with their fathers in the day I took them by the hand to bring them out of the land of Egypt, My covenant which they broke, although I was a husband to them," declares the Lord. "But this is the covenant which I will make with the house of Israel after those days," declares the Lord, "I will put My law within them and on their heart I will write it; and I will be their God, and they shall be My people. . . . I will forgive their iniquity, and their sin I will remember no more." (Jer. 31:31–33, 34b)

What, precisely, does God's forgiveness do for us? "It removes all of the guilt and cause of alienation from the past, it assures a state of grace for the present, and it promises divine mercy and aid for the future. Its fullness cannot adequately be conveyed by any one term or formula."[7] What a precious gift Christ has secured for us!

Jesus' next words contained a sense of loss but also gave the disciples hope:

> "But I say to you, I will not drink of this fruit of the vine from now on until that day when I drink it new with you in My Father's kingdom." (Matt. 26:29)

Here is a magnificent allusion to the time when Christ will sit down at the great messianic banquet in His Father's kingdom—with all history consummated at the marriage supper of the Lamb (Rev. 19:7–9). As William Barclay concludes:

> Here, indeed, is divine faith and divine optimism. Jesus was going out to Gethsemane, out to trial before the Sanhedrin, out to the Cross—and yet *he is still*

---

7. William Charles Morro and Roland K. Harrison, "Forgiveness," in *The International Standard Bible Encyclopedia*, rev. ed., ed. Geoffrey W. Bromiley (1982; reprint, Grand Rapids, Mich.: William B. Eerdmans Publishing Co., 1987), vol. 2, p. 342.

thinking in terms of a Kingdom. To Jesus the Cross was never defeat; it was the way to glory. He was on his way to Calvary, but he was also on his way to a throne.[8]

How the Supper Ended

Matthew closes this scene in a quiet, reverent way:

> After singing a hymn, they went out to the Mount of Olives. (Matt. 26:30)

Maybe it took ten minutes, or even fifteen or twenty, for Jesus and His disciples to finish the Passover meal. Yet, regardless of how long it took, this meal swelled with eternal significance. Though once shrouded in mystery and ancient Jewish tradition, the Passover had been transformed to become, in Christian parlance, the ordinance of the Lord's Supper.

The disciples wouldn't fully realize this until later, but for now they sang with their Lord one of the traditional Passover hymns:[9]

> Give thanks to the Lord, for He is good;
> For His lovingkindness is everlasting.
> Oh Let Israel say,
> "His lovingkindness is everlasting."
> Oh let the house of Aaron say,
> "His lovingkindness is everlasting."
> Oh let those who fear the Lord say,
> "His lovingkindness is everlasting.". . .
> The stone which the builders rejected
> Has become the chief corner stone.
> This is the Lord's doing;
> It is marvelous in our eyes.
> This is the day which the Lord has made;
> Let us rejoice and be glad in it.
> O Lord, do save, we beseech You. . . .

8. William Barclay, *The Gospel of Matthew,* rev. ed., The Daily Study Bible Series (Philadelphia, Pa.: Westminster Press, 1975), vol. 2, pp. 342–43.

9. The hymns traditionally sung (antiphonally) at Passover were called the *Hallel,* or "hallelujah," psalms. Psalms 113 and possibly 114 were sung before the meal, and Psalms 115–118 were sung after the last cup. J. R. Sampey, "Hallel," in *The International Standard Bible Encyclopedia,* p. 600.

Blessed is the one who comes in the name of
the Lord;
We have blessed you from the house of the Lord.
The Lord is God, and He has given us light. . . .
Give thanks to the Lord, for He is good;
For His lovingkindness is everlasting.
(Ps. 118:1–4, 22–25a, 26–27a, 29)

Each time we gather around the bread and the cup to make confession of sin, to eat the bread and drink from the cup, and sing our hymns of trust, we do so in remembrance of Him . . . and the death He died so that we could live. And our hearts sing anew the glorious truth that:

Jesus paid it all,
All to Him I owe;
Sin had left a crimson stain—
He washed it white as snow.[10]

 ## Living Insights

Take a moment to remember the last time you celebrated the Lord's Supper. Was it tacked on to an already crowded worship schedule, giving the impression that it wasn't very important? Was it so shrouded in symbolism and mystery that the simple message of thanksgiving disappeared in the pomp and circumstance? Or were your mind and heart distracted by all the things you needed to get done that day or in the coming week?

Take some time to reflect on the true significance of the Lord's Supper to you as a believer in Christ, so that the next time you celebrate communion you can have a deeply meaningful time of worship.

Read through 1 Corinthians 11:23–32. In what ways is communion an act of personal worship? What preparation is needed? Why?

_____

_____

_____

10. Elvina M. Hall, "Jesus Paid It All," in _The Hymnal for Worship and Celebration_ (Waco, Tex.: Word Music, 1986), no. 210.

How does participating in the Lord's Supper "proclaim" Christ's death? How does that add to the significance of communion for you personally?

_____

_____

_____

_____

Next, read 1 Corinthians 10:16–17. What do you think it means to participate, or "share," in the blood and body of Christ (see also Rom. 6:2–8; 8:1–2, 32–39; Eph. 1:3–14; 2:12–22; Col. 1:19–23; Heb. 10:19–22; 1 John 1:7)?

_____

_____

_____

_____

How is the Lord's Supper connected with the unity of His body, the church (1 Cor. 10:17; 11:20–22, 33–34)? How can caring for our unity be part of preparation for communion, and how much is unity an expression of communion (see Eph. 4:1–3; 4:25–5:2)?

_____

_____

_____

_____

Now list some of the things you will do in preparation for celebrating the Lord's Supper in order to make it a more worshipful and Christ-honoring time.

_____

_____

_____

_____

Finally, take some time to go to the Lord in prayer. In the most honest, direct words possible, express your gratitude to Him for what He accomplished for you in His death. Then renew your commitment to live in a way that pleases Him.

 ## Questions for Group Reflection

> And when He had given thanks, He broke it and said, "This is My body, which is for you; do this in remberance of Me." In the same way He took the cup also after the supper, saying, "This cup is the new covenant in My blood; do this, as often as you drink it, in remembrance of Me." (1 Corinthians 11:24–25)

> And when He had taken some break and given thanks, He broke it and gave it to them, saying, "This is My body which is given for you; do this in remembrance of Me." And in the same way He took the cup after they had eaten, saying, "This cup which is poured out for you is the new covenant in My blood." (Luke 22:19–20)

1. Paul and Luke both record Jesus adding the words "Do this in remembrance of Me" to His directions to "Take, eat" and "Drink from it, all of you" (1 Cor. 11:24–25; Luke 22:19). What do you think is involved in remembering Christ?

2. How is communion with the Lord also communion with each other?

3. Jesus' last meal on earth was a time of intimacy and betrayal, gratitude and grief, deliverance accomplished and sacrifice soon to come. The bread was broken and the wine poured out, and in only hours Jesus' body would be broken and His life poured out on the cross. For us. For the forgiveness of our sins. For our peace with God. For our eternal life. What thoughts come to your mind as you ponder the meaning of the bread and the cup?

4. Come before the Lord in prayer now, thanking Him for the significance of the bread and the cup and asking Him to give you a renewed sense of awe for Him and His work on the cross.

Chapter 3

MIDNIGHT IN THE GARDEN
Mark 14:32–42

Huntsville, Texas, is no Garden of Gethsemane. But the two sites share a strange distinction. They're places where the condemned have prepared to die. Humanness distills to its rawest state in the final hours before execution . . . there's nothing frivolous, no frittering away of life's final moments. Only an individual, alone with his soul, doing what seems best at the time to ready himself for eternity.

In Huntsville, the town where Texas houses and executes death-row criminals, hundreds of inmates have spent their waning hours of life preparing for certain death. Many find religion and spend their time reading the Bible and talking with spiritual advisors. Others write to friends and family, leaving lasting testaments for those who matter most. Some, hardened by a life of crime, go through the hours eerily defiant and mysteriously calm.

Whatever the case, humanity is on full display. It was the same in the Garden of Gethsemane, where Jesus prepared to die. Perhaps more than in any other scene in Scripture, we observe His humanity here . . . in the last, haunting hours of His life. Thankfully, the gospel painter resisted airbrushing away the agonizing evidence of Christ's vigil. Instead, we find Him alone, trembling, surrounded by only a few sleepy disciples, and desperately praying.

Does God *really* know what it's like to be human? Gethsemane removes all doubt.

The Place of Prayer

Mark 14:32–42 represents only a snapshot from a larger view of Christ's Passion (His life from the Last Supper to the grave). In fact, the Passion narratives in the Gospels make up "the longest consecutive action recounted of Jesus."[1] And "nearly half of each Gospel is devoted to the story of Jesus' death. The Gospels have

---

1. Raymond E. Brown, *The Death of the Messiah: From Gethsemane to the Grave* (New York, N.Y.: Doubleday, 1994), vol. 1, p. i.

appropriately been described as passion narratives with extended introductions."[2]

These narratives have been the stuff of playwrights and poets, pedagogues and pulpiteers through the ages by sheer virtue of the human drama they depict. In Gethsemane we see a human Jesus, perhaps more than in any other scene in Scripture. This particular scene opens with Jesus retreating to a secluded place to engage in a rite purely human:

> They came to a place named Gethsemane; and He said to His disciples, "Sit here until I have prayed." (Mark 14:32)

Sometime nearing midnight, Jesus and His disciples arrived in this secluded, gardenlike place—most likely a privately owned grove of olive trees—where He came often to pray. Gethsemane was located on the slope of the Mount of Olives,[3] and the name literally means "oil press," from the Greek word *Gethsemanei*,[4] suggesting the presence of an olive press nearby.

Before going off alone to pray, Jesus instructed His disciples to sit and wait, possibly as guards to the entrance of the garden but also as witnesses to His time of prayer (compare 13:32–37). Instead of going off completely alone, however, He invited three of His closest companions to journey deeper into the garden.

> And He took with Him Peter and James and John, and began to be very distressed and troubled. And He said to them, "My soul is deeply grieved to the point of death; remain here and keep watch." (14:33–34)

Jesus didn't wish to endure this ordeal in solitude. He knew what suffering awaited Him in Jerusalem, and the sheer horror of those thoughts gripped Him to the point that, according to Mark, He became "very distressed" and "troubled." Both terms express inner turmoil and mounting anxiety. Alone with those to whom

2. T. Desmond Alexander and Brian S. Rosner, eds., *New Dictionary of Biblical Theology* (Downers Grove, Ill.: InterVarsity Press, 2000). See Part Two: Biblical Corpora and Books, article on "The Synoptic Gospels," section on "The Centrality of the Passion."

3. W. W. Gasque, "Gethsemane," in *The International Standard Bible Encyclopedia*, rev. ed., ed. Geoffrey W. Bromiley (1982; reprint, Grand Rapids, Mich.: William B. Eerdmans Publishing Co., 1987), vol. 2, p. 457.

4. Brown, *The Death of the Messiah*, p. 148.

He was closest, Jesus cracked open a window to His troubled soul and confessed that it was "deeply grieved" (see Isa. 53:3a).

Perhaps Judas' defection and betrayal, Peter's foreseen denial, the abuse He would endure at the hands of Roman soldiers, and ultimately, the certain torture of the cross had conspired against Jesus' peaceful resolve. Until now we've seen a steady, calm, and deliberate Jesus. Now we view an anxious, troubled, even terrorized Jesus, leaning hard on the support of His closest companions.

The Movement of Submission

> And He went a little beyond them, and fell to the ground and began to pray. (Mark 14:35a)

The verb in the Greek phrase translated "*fell* to the ground" is in the imperfect tense, suggesting a continual action. In other words, Jesus literally kept falling to the ground in prayer, crying out to His Father, then rising to His feet, only to fall again to the ground in prayer.

Portraits of a serene Jesus kneeling beside a rock, crowned in moonlight, mislead us. Mark described a Jesus wrestling with His destiny, pacing, falling to the ground, desperately petitioning the Father for relief, and entreating Him as a young son would his daddy:

> "Abba! Father!" (v. 36a)

Jesus called God "Abba," an extremely intimate word—one not even the most pious Jew would utter for fear of offending the Lord. Jesus, however, deliberately invoked His Father's most intimate, tender name and made a startling request:

> [He] began to pray that if it were possible, the hour might pass Him by. And He was saying, "Abba! Father! All things are possible for You; remove this cup from Me; yet not what I will, but what You will." (vv. 35b–36)

How could this be? The Son of God desired relief from His divine commission? Here in Gethsemane, Jesus seemed squeezed, pressed between duty and desire. Yet, despite feeling the weight of the world's sin pressing down on Him, He willingly accepted His cup. D. A. Carson explains:

> The wrath of God was turned loose on Him. Only

this can adequately explain what happened in Gethsemane. . . . Jesus believed that with God anything was possible and therefore prayed for the cup to be removed from him. This cup is the same one Jesus referred to in [Mark] 10:38–39—the cup of the wrath of God . . . a metaphor of punishment and judgment. Here it obviously refers to Jesus' death. Jesus' desire was for the removal of the cup. But he willingly placed his will in submission to his Father's will.[5]

When Jesus returned to His small group of disciples, He found them not alert and waiting, but dozing in the darkness:

And He came and found them sleeping, and said to Peter, "Simon, are you asleep? Could you not keep watch for one hour? Keep watching and praying that you may not come into temptation; the spirit is willing, but the flesh is weak." (Mark 14:37–38)

Dismayed, Jesus spoke directly to Peter using his former name, "Simon"—a gesture perhaps intended as a subtle rebuke (he wasn't exactly behaving like the "rock" Jesus needed him to be [see Matt. 16:18]). Ironically, Peter, who had not long before boasted a to-the-death allegiance to Christ, surrendered to his body's demands for sleep. Craig S. Keener notes that "it was customary to stay awake late on Passover night and to speak of God's redemption. The disciples should have been able to stay awake to keep watch; they had probably stayed up late on nearly every other Passover of their lives."[6]

Jesus repeated His earlier command "to watch and pray" and added a warning concerning temptation, an ominous admonition to steel themselves for the certain danger of defection ahead.

Remarkably, not even Jesus, Lord of the universe, could skirt

---

5. D. A. Carson, "Mark," in *The Expositor's Bible Commentary*, ed. Frank E. Gaebelein (Grand Rapids, Mich.: Zondervan Publishing House, 1984), vol. 8, pp. 763–64.

6. T. Desmond Alexander and Brian S. Rosner, eds., *New Dictionary of Biblical Theology* (Downers Grove, Ill.: InterVarsity Press, 2000). See Part Three: Biblical Themes, article on "Obedience," section on "The Obedience of Jesus Christ." Gethsemane also "shares something important with the original Paradise: it is a sacred space within which a radical decision is made that reverses the course of human history." Leland Ryken, James C. Wilhoit, and Tremper Longman III, *Dictionary of Biblical Imagery* (Downers Grove, Ill.: InterVarsity Press, 2000). See "Garden."

the necessity of prayer to ready Himself for the grueling responsibility of the Cross:

> Again He went away and prayed, saying the same words. And again He came and found them sleeping, for their eyes were very heavy; and they did not know what to answer Him. (Mark 14:39–40)

Jesus returned to the still-sleeping disciples, now speechless in their embarrassment. Then, coming back for a third time, He found nothing had changed:

> And He came the third time, and said to them, "Are you still sleeping and resting? It is enough; the hour has come; behold, the Son of Man is being betrayed into the hands of sinners. Get up, let us be going; behold, the one who betrays Me is at hand!" (vv. 41–42).

Jesus roused the disciples from their slumbering. As they stumbled up, Jesus resolved that "the hour [had] come," and He turned to face His destiny. This was God's plan. There was no escaping it. Betrayal was at hand.

The Bitter Cup

This scene did not end peacefully. Mark says, "Immediately while He was still speaking . . . (v. 43)." Jesus hadn't even finished His last sentence, when:

> Judas, one of the twelve, came up accompanied by a crowd with swords and clubs, who were from the chief priests and the scribes and the elders. Now he who was betraying Him had given them a signal, saying, "Whomever I kiss, He is the one; seize Him and lead Him away under guard." After coming, Judas immediately went to Him, saying, "Rabbi!" and kissed Him. They laid hands on Him and seized Him. But one of those who stood by drew his sword, and struck the slave of the high priest and cut off his ear. And Jesus said to them, "Have you come out with swords and clubs to arrest Me, as you would against a robber? Every day I was with you in the temple teaching, and you did not seize Me; but this

has taken place to fulfill the Scriptures." And they all left Him and fled. (vv. 43–50; see also Matt. 26:47–56; Luke 22:47–53; John 18:3–12)

Weakened by fear, Jesus' disciples scattered into the cover of night like helpless animals fleeing a lioness on her midnight prowl. And Jesus was left to face His accusers alone.

Gethsemane reminds us of another garden—the Garden of Eden, where the first man, Adam, was not willing to submit his will to the Father (Gen. 3). Adam's "disobedience lost life with God for all his descendants"; but Jesus' obedience, hard-won as it was, gives us "the gift of righteousness, guaranteeing glory, [and] comes to all who are linked with him by faith."[7] Or as Paul put it:

> For as through one man's disobedience the many were made sinners, even so through the obedience of the One the many will be made righteous. (Rom. 5:19)

So, we know that ultimately good came from this gloomy end. But resist the urge to jump ahead; instead, linger in this moment with Christ, and consider what He chose to do for you.

 Living Insights

In his devotional titled *Intense Moments with the Savior*, writer Ken Gire composed a beautiful meditation focusing on the Gethsemane scene:

> Jesus pushes himself up from the ground and lifts his eyes towards heaven.
> "Yet not what I will, but what you will."
> His hands are no longer clutching the grass in despair. They are no longer clasping each other in prayer.
> They are raised toward heaven.
> Reaching not for bread or for fish or for any other good gift. Not even for answers.
> But reaching for the cup from his Father's hand.

7. Craig S. Keener, *IVP Bible Background Commentary: New Testament* (Downers Grove, Ill.: InterVarsity Press, 1997). See Mark 14:32–34.

> And though it is a terrible cup, brimming with
> the wrath of God for the ferment of sin from cen-
> turies past and centuries yet to come . . . and
> though it is a cup he fears . . . he takes it.
> Because more than he fears the cup, he loves
> the hand from which it comes.[8]

Love for the Father and obedience to His will go hand in hand. What motivated Jesus and what should compel us to surrender to God's plan for our own lives is love for Him.

What gets in the way of that obedience is our humanity, or our love for self. Numerous aspects of human nature tempt us away from faithful obedience to the Lord. Here are a few that come to mind:

- A need to satisfy fleshy desires (lust)

- A natural resourcefulness (self-sufficiency)

- A careless embracing of worldly wisdom (capitulation)

- A fear of failure or rejection (inferiority)

- A bent toward self-preservation (fear)

- A stubborn insistence for control and recognition (pride)

- A refusal to separate from family or friends (dependency)

- A bottomless appetite for comfort and ease (materialism)

These are only a few. You could probably list others. The point is, left to ourselves, we usually find sufficient reason to wiggle out of fully accepting God's plan for our lives. But, with Jesus Christ as our example, we can learn to obey and to embrace it.

Consider the following verse as you answer the questions that follow.

> Therefore, when He comes into the world, He says,
> "Sacrifice and offering You have not desired,
> But a body You have prepared for Me;
> In whole burnt offerings and sacrifices for sin You
>   have taken no pleasure.
> Then I said, 'Behold, I have come (in the scroll of

8. Ken Gire, *Intense Moments with the Savior: Learning to Feel* (Grand Rapids, Mich.: Zonder-van Publishing House, 1994), p. 85.

the book it is written of Me) to do your will, O God.'" (Heb. 10:5–7)

Do you struggle with God's will for your life? What aspects of His will are you having difficulty accepting? Be specific.

_____

_____

_____

_____

_____

_____

Have there been times in your life when you had determined to follow the Lord and then were beset by human weaknesses, such as fear, pride, or lack of patience? If so, describe some of those times.

_____

_____

_____

_____

_____

_____

What role does prayer play in helping you trust God's way rather than your own? How would you describe your attitude toward prayer as it pertains to being obedient to God's will?

_____

_____

_____

_____

If you were to place yourself in the Gethsemane story, who would you be? A sleepy disciple, following Christ only until it cost you something? A doubting, manipulating Judas, concerned only about financial prosperity? Or Jesus, though fully human, totally surrendered to God's will?

_____

_____

_____

_____

_____

Let's pray.

> Dear Man of Sorrows,
> Thank you for Gethsemane. For a place to go when there's no place to go but God. For a place to pray. And to cry. And to find out who I really am underneath the rhetoric.
> I know that sometime, somewhere, some type of Gethsemane awaits me. Just as it did you. I know that someday a dark night will fall upon my soul. Just as it did for yours. But I shudder to think about it, about the darkness and the aloneness and the despair.
> Prepare me for that dark night, Lord. Prepare me now by helping me realize that although Gethsemane is the most terrifying of places, it is also the most tranquil.
> The terror comes in realizing I am not in control of my life or the lives of those I love. The tranquility comes in realizing that you are.
> Help me when it is dark and I am alone and afraid. Help me to put my trembling hand in yours and trust you with my life. And with the lives of those I love.
> Someday I know I will wrestle with the circumstances that are beyond my control, that some sort of suffering will pin me to the cold, hard ground.
> When that happens, Lord Jesus, help me to realize that the victories of heaven are the defeats of the human soul. And that my strength is not found in how courageously I struggle but in how completely I surrender . . .[9]

9. Gire, *Intense Moments with the Savior*, p. 86.

Questions for Group Reflection

1. Do you think Jesus really wanted to avoid going to the cross, to get out of the mission God had sent Him on? Why or why not?

2. Why do you think the gospel writers (via the Holy Spirit) included this scene from Gethsemane? What was Jesus showing us here? How do Hebrews 5:8, Romans 5:19, and Revelation 21:5 shed light on this question?

3. What have you learned about your Lord and about yourself from this encounter with Christ?

4. Spend some time together in prayer now, sharing with the Father the thoughts and feelings that arise as you consider Gethsemane and asking for our "Abba's" grace to follow in Jesus' obedient steps.

Chapter 4

THREE O'CLOCK IN THE MORNING

Mark 14:27–31, 53–54, 66–72

You younger men, likewise, be subject to your elders;
and all of you, clothe yourselves with humility toward one another, for God is opposed to the proud,
but gives grace to the humble.
Therefore humble yourselves under the mighty
hand of God, that He may exalt you at the proper
time. (1 Pet. 5:5–6)

Those verses, which represent some of the most tender words in
the Bible, were penned by one who once knew little of humility. Peter, the audacious, tough-skinned, broad-shouldered Galilean, had courageously, though presumptuously, pledged a fighting
allegiance to Christ. But before that bold resolve had opportunity
to shine, it quickly melted in the glow of a Roman campfire. Spiritually collapsed, Peter had to come to grips with his own weakness.

Solomon wrote, "Humility goes before honor" (Prov. 18:12)—
a lesson Peter and the other disciples learned the hard way. Mark 14
contains a poignant story of courage and cowardice, of determina-
tion and denial. As we study, we'll have an opportunity to test our
own loyalty to the Savior and wonder anew with the hymnist of old:

Must Jesus bear the cross alone
And all the world go free?[1]

A Painful Prediction

By now, the disciples had grown accustomed to hearing Jesus
make odd, often shocking statements. But nothing could have prepared them for this alarming prediction:

And Jesus said to them, "You will all fall away,
because it is written, 'I will strike down the shepherd,

---

1. Thomas Shepherd and others, "Must Jesus Bear the Cross Alone?" in *The Hymnal for
Worship and Celebration* (Waco, Tex.: Word Music, 1986), no. 449.

and the sheep shall be scattered.' But after I have been raised, I will go ahead of you to Galilee." (Mark 14:27–28)

Jesus predicted total defection by His disciples. For the term *fall away*, He used a passive form of the Greek verb *skandalizo*, which means "to put a snare in the way" or "to cause to stumble." He knew that His arrest and subsequent suffering would rattle the disciples' resolve. But, as Walter Wessell notes, this does not mean "that the disciples will lose their faith in Jesus, but that their courage will fail and they will forsake him."[2]

Hope of Jesus reassembling His wayward flock in Galilee after His resurrection (which surely must have been another puzzling reference for the disciples), however, tempered the grim news of their scandalized, tripped-up faith.

A contest of predictions and counterpredictions between Peter and Jesus followed:

> But Peter said to Him, "Even though all may fall away, yet I will not." And Jesus said to him, "Truly I say to you, that this very night, before a rooster crows twice, you yourself will deny Me three times." (Mark 14:29–30)

Not only would Peter fall away, but that "very night" he would deny Jesus "three times" before cockcrow.[3]

The precision of Jesus' prediction only fueled Peter's protest:

> But Peter kept saying insistently, "Even if I have to die with You, I will not deny You!" And they all were saying the same thing also. (Mark 14: 31)

Another to-the-death pronouncement of allegiance to Jesus sounded from the ranks. However, as night gave way to early

---

2. Walter W. Wessell, "Mark," in *The Expositor's Bible Commentary*, ed. Frank E. Gaebelein (Grand Rapids, Mich.: Zondervan Publishing House, 1984), vol. 8, p. 762.

3. This likely refers to the third watch of night known by the Jews as *cockcrowing* (3:00 A.M. to 6:00 A.M.). "The reference to the cock crowing may be to the actual bird or to the blast of the Roman trumpets that marked that time of night. . . . The Roman bugle call at 3:00 A.M. . . . was known as *gallicinium*." R. Alan Cole, "Mark," and I. Howard Marshall, "Luke," in *New Bible Commentary: 21st Century Edition*, 4th ed., rev., ed. D. A. Carson and others (Downers Grove, Ill.: InterVarsity Press, 1994), pp. 972, 1016. Marshall believes it was, in fact, a literal rooster.

dawn, the disciples' bravely proclaimed loyalty evaporated with the morning dew.

Falling away from Christ

Jesus' predictions hit the mark. Following Judas' betrayal of Jesus (vv. 10–11, 18–21, 43–50) the disciples' ranks thinned quickly. Finally, there were none. Jesus *would* in fact bear the cross alone. Mark states simply:

> And they all left Him and fled. (v. 50)

Though the rest fled the scene completely, Mark tells us that Peter stayed in the shadows:

> They led Jesus away to the high priest; and all the chief priests and the elders and the scribes gathered together. Peter had followed Him at a distance, right into the courtyard of the high priest; and he was sitting with the officers and warming himself by the fire. (vv. 53–54)

Peter was not standing alongside Jesus as he had so boldly sworn he would do. However, from where he sat, he no doubt could see Jesus and hear what was going on around Him. It's difficult to imagine what was going on in Peter's mind as he watched Jesus endure lashing ridicule and persecution from His captors. Mark provides some of the details (details that most likely came from Peter himself):

> Some began to spit at Him, and to blindfold Him, and to beat Him with their fists, and to say to Him, "Prophesy!" And the officers received Him with slaps in the face. (v. 65)

From here, the scene goes from bad to worse.

Peter's Tragic Denials

> As Peter was below in the courtyard, one of the servant-girls of the high priest came, and seeing Peter warming himself, she looked at him and said, "You also were with Jesus the Nazarene." (vv. 66–67)

Peter's response to being recognized chills the soul:

> But he denied it, saying, "I neither know nor under-
> stand what you are talking about." And he went out
> onto the porch, and a rooster crowed. (v. 68)

Peter's resolve vanished as the first denial fell from his lips. The
woman continued to press him:

> The servant-girl saw him, and began once more to
> say to the bystanders, "This is one of them!" But
> again he denied it. (vv. 69–70a)

Denial number two. And it wasn't over yet:

> And after a little while the bystanders were again
> saying to Peter, "Surely you are one of them, for you
> are a Galilean too." But he began to curse and swear,
> "I do not know this man you are talking about!"
> (vv. 70b–71)

Apparently, Peter's accent betrayed his Galilean roots (see
Matt. 26:73). Feeling cornered, he swore by an oath that he absolutely didn't know Jesus at all.[4] Jesus' prophecy was now fulfilled:

> Immediately a rooster crowed a second time. And
> Peter remembered how Jesus had made the remark to
> him, "Before a rooster crows twice, you will deny Me
> three times." And he began to weep. (Mark 14:72)

Peter's heart swelled with regret as the second cockcrow sounded
in the night. It was over. Three denials, a pained look from Jesus
(see Luke 22:61) . . . and chapter 14 leaves Peter somewhere in
Jerusalem alone with his tears.

Some Concluding Thoughts

How could such brave resolve melt into complete denial? Most
likely, fear overwhelmed Peter's heart. Peter and the others found
quite appealing the idea of following Christ in the spotlight of
public acclaim. A certain thrill accompanied being seen with Jesus.

---

4. Gerhard Kittel and Gerhard Friedrich, eds., *Theological Dictionary of the New Testament*,
translated and abridged in one volume by Geoffrey W. Bromiley (1985; reprint, Grand Rapids,
Mich.: William B. Eerdmans Publishing Co., 1992), pp. 57, 683–84.

But when things got dicey, when the tables turned, and their lives were on the line, their faith legs got wobbly.

Mark's point rings clear: Following Christ is no easy life. It will probably cost you everything.

Explore that thought further in the Living Insights section that follows. But before you do, pause a moment to reflect on Peter's failure and the remorse he surely experienced having denied His friend and Savior.

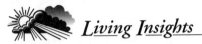 *Living Insights*

Mark 14:27–31 makes it clear that those who think the Christian life is a cakewalk had better think again! Bible commentator Raymond Brown notes:

> Mark takes very seriously the saying quoted in [Mark] 8:34 that following Jesus involves taking up the cross, and Mark does not wish the reader to be deceived about the difficulty of that task. When the disciples of Jesus who had walked with him most intimately, who indeed had already begun their following of him, faced the issue of accompanying him to the cross, they were scandalized and even denied him. Peter in particular underestimated the trial that faced him ("Even if all . . . yet not I"), and he led all the others to state assuredly that they would not be scandalized.[5]

As we noted earlier in this chapter, in Mark 14:27, "falling away" doesn't mean to lose our faith but to shrink back when outside forces threaten our faith. To "take up our cross and follow" (8:27) Christ means total commitment to Him in every aspect of our lives. And often that involves risk.

Most of us may never face a literal life-or-death decision with regard to standing for Christ. But we all meet up with opportunities to witness to our trust in Him. Those opportunities are lost, and we, in effect, deny Christ when fear pins us to the ground.

---

5. Raymond E. Brown, *The Death of the Messiah: From Gethsemane to the Grave* (New York, N.Y.: Doubleday, 1994), vol. 1, p. 141.

Can you describe a time when fear kept you from representing your faith in Christ? Describe the situation and how you handled it. How did you feel?

_____

_____

_____

_____

_____

How can times of adversity provide opportunities to witness to our trust in the Lord?

_____

_____

_____

_____

What are some ways we "deny" Christ in our daily lives?

_____

_____

_____

How often do you share your faith in Jesus? How do fear of rejection and feelings of inadequacy hinder a vibrant witness?

_____

_____

_____

_____

What would it take for you to overcome your fear of sharing your faith? Circle all that apply.

   a. greater knowledge of the Scriptures

   b. some evangelism training

   c. a prayer support group

   d. a convicting sermon

What steps are you willing to take to shore up some of these areas of your Christian life? Be specific.

_____

_____

_____

_____

Take some time to read over the following Bible passages:

Matthew 28:18–20	1 Corinthians 2:3–5
John 14:26–27	2 Corinthians 1:5–11
Acts 1:8	2 Corinthians 4:7–10
Romans 1:16–17	Ephesians 6:10–13

How do these verses provide help in our struggle to remain faithful to Christ? What resources has the Lord provided to help us avoid "falling away"?

_____

_____

_____

_____

_____

Close your time in the Scriptures today in prayer. Be very honest with the Lord about your fears and doubts, especially as they relate to witnessing. Pray for boldness to share your faith with friends and family members who need Christ. Ask Him to strengthen you and to help you take up *your* cross today, though so many have gone weak in the knees. Then, thank Him for His abundant supply of grace and forgiveness and that His strength is made perfect in weakness.

Quietly ponder the remaining words of this hymn:

> Must Jesus bear the cross alone
> And all the world go free?
> No, there's a cross for ev'ryone,
> And there's a cross for me![6]

And . . . thee!

 Questions for Group Reflection

1. "Even if I have to die with You," Peter insisted, "I will not deny You!" What scenario might Peter have had in mind when he told Jesus this (compare Luke 22:35–38; John 18:10)? What do you think was at the heart of his struggle?

2. Which is easier: fighting for Christ or following Him into suffering? Why? Have you ever faced Peter's dilemma in your own life? How did you fare?

3. Fortunately, the denial wasn't the end of Peter's life or ministry. On the morning of Jesus' Resurrection, the angel at the empty tomb told the amazed women to go and tell His disciples—and he specifically singled out Peter (Mark 16:7). Jesus later fully restored him, giving Peter three opportunities to affirm his love for Him and thereby redeem his three denials (read aloud John 21:15–17). What do these scenes from Mark and John tell you about our Lord and about our own failures?

4. Come together now to support one another in prayer. Thank the Lord Jesus Christ for being willing to go to the cross alone. Thank Him for His love for Peter and for us. Thank Him for His restoring grace. Thank Him for whatever it is that you, personally, feel grateful for today.

---

6. Shepherd, "Must Jesus Bear the Cross Alone?", no. 449.

Chapter 5

THE SIX TRIALS OF JESUS

Selected Scripture

M ost of us can handle the jabs that life's little hardships deliver. But how difficult it is to endure the crushing blows of injustice. When unfair treatment blindsides us, our whole world starts spinning in a blur of inequities. Everything solid turns to sand. The legal system fails us. Longtime friends eye us with uncertainty. Then there are the inner ragings—anger steals away our sleep, thoughts of revenge and bouts of depression rob us of joy, while doubt darkens our soul. Finally, we cry out to God like the prophet Habakkuk:

> How long, O Lord, will I call for help,
> And You will not hear? (Hab. 1:2a)

We're stopped cold, though, when we remember the words of Isaiah 53:

> He was oppressed and He was afflicted,
> Yet He did not open His mouth;
> Like a lamb that is led to slaughter,
> And like a sheep that is silent before its shearers,
> So He did not open His mouth.
> By oppression and judgment He was taken away.
> (vv. 7–8a)

Having endured the scourge of injustice, Jesus looks on our pain and confusion with understanding eyes. So, when we bring those injustices to the Savior, we experience a depth of oneness with Him never before felt. And instead of finding a list of answers, we end our search in an embrace of love.

The gospel writers include remarkable details about the six trials of Jesus that led to His violent death on the cross—heartrending details that flesh out the oppression, affliction, and wrongful judgment Isaiah's Lamb suffered. By watching Jesus calmly endure this frenzied sequence of travesties, we can find strength and comfort to stand firm in our faith when injustice rips at our soul.

This chapter has been adapted from "A Closer Look at Jesus' Arrest and Trials," in the Bible study guide *A Look at the Book*, by Lee Hough and Bryce Klabunde, from the Bible-teaching ministry of Charles R. Swindoll (Anaheim, Calif.: Charles R. Swindoll, Inc., 1994).

The Matter of Time

The timing of Jesus' arrest and trials generates much confusion. To clear the fog, we need a better grasp of the way the Jewish people of that day reckoned time. The start and end of a twenty-four-hour day in the New Testament differed from ours today. While our day runs from midnight to midnight, their day ran from 6:00 A.M. to 6:00 P.M.

Their days and nights were divided uniquely as well. Sections of time through the night were distinguished by *watches*, which were three-hour time segments. Nighttime consisted of four watches: the "first watch," 6:00 P.M. to 9:00 P.M.; the "second watch," 9:00 P.M. to midnight; the "third watch," midnight to 3:00 A.M.; and the "fourth watch," 3:00 A.M. to 6:00 A.M. Daytime began at 6:00 A.M. and was divided into twelve individual hours. For example, the "third hour" would have been 9:00 A.M., and the "ninth hour" would have been 3:00 P.M.

Understanding these distinctions helps us realize the ceaseless cruelty Jesus endured during His final day on earth.

Chronology of Events

Wave after wave of treachery and deceit swept over Jesus with relentless intensity, giving Him no relief, no time to catch His breath and recover. The following chart demonstrates the sequence of events.

CHRONOLOGY OF EVENTS	
EVENT	APPROXIMATE TIME
Prayer and agony at Gethsemane (Matthew, Mark, Luke)	1:00 A.M.
Betrayal by Judas and arrest of Jesus (Mark 14:43–46; John 18:12)	1:30 A.M.
Irregular, unauthorized inquiry at Annas' residence (John 18:13–23)	2:00 A.M.
Unofficial trial at Caiaphas' residence (Matthew 26:57–68; John 18:24	3:30 A.M.
Formal, official trial before Sanhedrin in their chamber to confirm capital sentence (Mark 15:1; Luke 22:66–71)	6:00 A.M. ("when it was day")

First interrogation by Pilate at official residence (Matthew 27:1–2, 11–14; Luke 23:1–7; John 18:28–38)	6:30 A.M. ("when morning had come . . . and it was early")
Audience/mockery before Herod (Luke 23:8–12)	7:00 A.M.
Final judgment of Pilate (All Gospels)	7:30 A.M.
Scourging in Praetorium (All Gospels)	8:00 A.M.
Nailing of hands and feet to the cross (All Gospels)	9:00 A.M. ("it was the third hour")
Darkness (Matthew, Mark, Luke)	12:00 Noon ("when the sixth hour had come, darkness fell")
Death of Jesus (All Gospels)	3:00 P.M. ("and at the ninth hour")

In less than twenty-four hours, Jesus goes from arrest to execution.

The Six Trials of Jesus

Following His arrest, Jesus was dragged from the Garden of Gethsemane across the Kidron valley into Jerusalem. No longer free, He had become property of the state and would be railroaded through the most fallacious, unfair, disorderly, illegal series of trials in the history of religious and civil jurisprudence.[1]

Between 2:00 A.M. and 7:30 A.M., Jesus was subjected to not one but six trials—three Jewish, three Roman. The religious leaders initially charged Jesus with blasphemy. But, since the Jewish people were not allowed to administer capital punishment, they changed the charge to treason, punishable by crucifixion under Roman law. Let's take a closer look at these six trials.

The First Trial: Jesus before Annas

Jesus' first trial transpired illegally during the hours of darkness in the home of Annas. Father-in-law of the high priest, Caiaphas

---

1. For an overview of the various illegal aspects of Jesus' six trials, see the chart at the end of this chapter.

and a former high priest himself, Annas was a wealthy and influential man of the city (see John 18:13). He served as somewhat of a high priest emeritus, enjoying remarkable influence over Roman rule.

As Jesus stood fettered meekly before him, Annas gloatingly interrogated Him on two counts: His teaching and His disciples (v. 19). Jesus' unflinching response put the legal burden of proof back on Annas' shoulders, where it belonged:

> "I have spoken openly to the world; I always taught in synagogues and in the temple, where all the Jews come together; and I spoke nothing in secret. Why do you question Me? Question those who have heard what I spoke to them; they know what I said." (vv. 20–21)

This kangaroo court could not have rendered a more inappropriate response:

> When He had said this, one of the officers standing nearby struck Jesus, saying, "Is that the way You answer the high priest?" . . . So Annas sent Him bound to Caiaphas the high priest. (vv. 22, 24)

The Second Trial: Jesus before Caiaphas

Caiaphas shared Annas' corrupt nature but not his cleverness. Jesus was brought to him illegally in the wee hours of the night, but Caiaphas allowed the trial to proceed anyway. As the ruling member of the Sanhedrin, he was responsible for ensuring a fair trial, but justice wasn't what he was after:

> Now the chief priests and the whole Council kept trying to obtain false testimony against Jesus, so that they might put Him to death. They did not find any, even though many false witnesses came forward. (Matt. 26:59–60a)

Two false witnesses eventually came forward, but Jesus would not reply to their lies (vv. 60b–63a). Frustrated, Caiaphas turned to Jesus and demanded: "I adjure You by the living God, that You tell us whether You are the Christ, the Son of God" (v. 63b). Looking him dead in the eye, Jesus answered: "You have said it yourself; nevertheless I tell you, hereafter you will see the Son of Man sitting at the right hand of Power, and coming on the clouds of heaven" (v. 64).

At this, Caiaphas flew into a rage of religious ranting, commanding that the trial be cut short on the charge of blasphemy:

> Then the high priest tore his robes and said, "He has blasphemed! What further need do we have of witnesses? Behold, you have now heard the blasphemy; what do you think?" They answered, "He deserves death!"
>
> Then they spat in His face and beat Him with their fists; and others slapped Him, and said, "Prophesy to us, You Christ; who is the one who hit You?" (vv. 65–68)

The Third Trial: Jesus before the Council of Elders

In their violent rush to judgment, the religious rulers held a perfunctory meeting of the Sanhedrin, the seventy men who sat in ultimate authority over the Jewish people. In probably the shortest of the six trials, lasting no more than twenty to thirty minutes, they conducted their illegal business and reached a verdict:

> When it was day, the Council of elders of the people assembled, both chief priests and scribes, and they led Him away to their council chamber, saying, "If You are the Christ, tell us." But He said to them, "If I tell you, you will not believe; and if I ask a question, you will not answer. But from now on the Son of Man will be seated at the right hand of the power of God." And they all said, "Are You the Son of God, then?" And He said to them, "Yes, I am." Then they said, "What further need do we have of testimony? For we have heard it ourselves from His own mouth."
>
> Then the whole body of them got up and brought Him before Pilate. (Luke 22:66–23:1)

The Fourth Trial: Jesus before Pilate

Walter Liefeld provides some insight into the fourth trial:

> The trial now moves into its Roman phase. While there had doubtless been more interrogation than the [Synoptic Gospels] report before Pilate declared he found no basis for a charge against Jesus (v. 4), it obviously did not take Pilate long to determine Jesus'

innocence. The larger part of this section deals, not with the trial as such, but with the difficulty the authorities had in trying to convict an innocent man.[2]

Roman law prohibited the Jewish people from putting someone to death, so they sent Jesus before Pontius Pilate under the charge of treason. At this time, Pilate served as governor of Judea, an ill-fitted post for a man known to be sarcastic, unsympathetic, and antagonistic toward the Jewish people. Ironically, he was vulnerable because of a clause in Roman jurisdiction that allowed the Jewish people to report any mistreatment by him to the emperor.[3]

The religious leaders had only to turn up the political heat to get Pilate to rule their way.[4] Following a brief dialogue between Pilate, the priests, and the scribes (John 18:28–32), Pilate turned to the accused:

> So Pilate asked Him, saying, "Are You the King of the Jews?" And He answered him and said, "It is as you say." Then Pilate said to the chief priests and the crowds, "I find no guilt in this man." (Luke 23:3–4)

However, Jesus' accusers would not be dissuaded.

> But they kept on insisting, saying, "He stirs up the people, teaching all over Judea, starting from Galilee even as far as this place." (v. 5)

Did someone say Galilee? That's all Pilate needed to hear. At last, he'd found a way to rid himself of this man. He promptly passed the buck to Herod, governor of Galilee, who happened to be in town on business:

> When Pilate heard it, he asked whether the man was a Galilean. And when he learned that He belonged to Herod's jurisdiction, he sent Him to Herod, who himself also was in Jerusalem at that time. (vv. 6–7)

---

2. Walter L. Leifeld, "Luke," in *The Expositor's Bible Commentary*, ed. Frank E. Gaebelein (Grand Rapids, Mich.: Zondervan Publishing House, 1984), vol. 8, p. 1039.

3. See William Barclay, *The Gospel of Matthew*, rev. ed., The Daily Study Bible Series (Philadelphia, Pa.: Westminster Press, 1975), vol. 2, pp. 358–59.

4. For a more detailed account of Jesus' trial before Pilate, see John 18:28–19:16.

The Fifth Trial: Jesus before Herod

Herod Antipas belonged to the notorious Herodian family—a Mafia-like regime known for its iniquitous rule. As tetrarch over Galilee between 4 B.C. and A.D. 39, he had ordered the beheading of John the Baptist (Matt. 14:1–12; Mark 6:16–29). Aware of his evil intentions, Jesus called him "that fox" in Luke 13:32. In fact, Herod was the one most likely to condemn Jesus to death. On this day, however, Herod was more intrigued by Jesus than intimidated by Him. And, for whatever reason, he wasn't in the killing mood:

> Now Herod was very glad when he saw Jesus; for he had wanted to see Him for a long time, because he had been hearing about Him and was hoping to see some sign performed by Him. (Luke 23:8)

Herod viewed Jesus more as a carnival sideshow than as an actual threat to the empire. Still, he felt obligated to question Jesus about the accusations leveled against Him:

> And he questioned Him at some length; but He answered him nothing. And the chief priests and the scribes were standing there, accusing Him vehemently. And Herod with his soldiers, after treating Him with contempt and mocking Him, dressed Him in a gorgeous robe and sent Him back to Pilate. Now Herod and Pilate became friends with one another that very day; for before they had been enemies with each other. (vv. 9–12)

In the face of raucous jesting and vulgar innuendoes, Jesus stood in regal dignity, silent and composed. Infuriated, His enemies wrapped Him in a kingly garment and returned Him to sender . . . without a conviction.

The Sixth Trial: Jesus before Pilate Again

A sharp rap on the door brought Pilate again face-to-face with the enigmatic Jesus. Still hoping to wiggle out of any decisive action, Pilate walked the tightrope between upholding justice and placating the crowd: he offered to rough up Jesus before releasing Him (vv. 13–16). But the crowd railed in protest (v. 18). Against a wall, Pilate tried one final route:

> Now at the feast the governor was accustomed

to release for the people any one prisoner whom they wanted. At that time they were holding a notorious prisoner, called Barabbas. So when the people gathered together, Pilate said to them, "Whom do you want me to release for you? Barabbas, or Jesus who is called Christ?" For he knew that because of envy they had handed Him over. (Matt. 27:15–18)

Pilate gambled that the crowd, which he found impervious to emotional appeal, would reason rationally in weighing the guilt of Barabbas, a violent insurrectionist who had committed murder (see Mark 15:7), against the innocence of Jesus. But Pilate lost the bet:

But the chief priests and the elders persuaded the crowds to ask for Barabbas and to put Jesus to death. But the governor said to them, "Which of the two do you want me to release for you?" And they said, "Barabbas." Pilate said to them, "Then what shall I do with Jesus who is called Christ?" They all said, "Crucify Him!" (Matt. 27:20–22)

Convinced he could not win this battle, Pilate "washed his hands in front of the crowd," telling the people, "I am innocent of this Man's blood; see to that yourselves" (v. 24)—as if that would somehow exonerate him of this final travesty. Yet, no matter how stubbornly he washed, the stain of his decision would follow him to his grave.

More shocking, though, was the crowd's response:

And all the people said, "His blood shall be on us and on our children!" (v. 25)

In a climactic final speech, Pilate again addressed the crowd:

Now it was the day of preparation for the Passover; it was about the sixth hour. And he said to the Jews, "Behold, your King!" (John 19:14)

The crowd, in a crazed crescendo, announced for all eternity its verdict:

So they cried out, "Away with Him, away with Him, crucify Him!" Pilate said to them, "Shall I crucify your King?" The chief priests answered, "We have

no king but Caesar." So he then handed Him over
to them to be crucified. (vv. 15–16)

The verdict was sealed for eternity. Unjustly condemned, the
Lamb of God was led to slaughter.

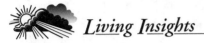 *Living Insights*

This study presents a remarkable paradox: *From acts of injustice,
the justice of God was satisfied.*

That's right. As humanity poured out its vicious wrath on Christ
at His trials and crucifixion, God's holy wrath against sin was completely released on Christ at the cross. The only barrier now separating a lost person from God is unbelief in Christ. Plain and simple.

Christ suffered and died for *you*. His death paid the price for
your sins. God will lovingly accept *you* into His family today if you
will accept His offer of forgiveness.

> If you confess with your mouth Jesus as Lord, and
> believe in your heart that God raised Him from the
> dead, you will be saved. (Rom. 10:9)

No strings attached. You believe in Him, and He will save you
from the penalty of your sin.

Is unbelief standing between you and God today? Perhaps you've
never thought Christ's sufferings and death were enough to pay the
price for your sins. What are you trying to add to them in an attempt
to satisfy God?

Spend some time reading through the following passages of
Scripture. As you do, allow God's truth to light a path for you from
the darkness of unbelief to the dawn of new life in His name!

John 3:16–17   1 Timothy 2:5–6

Romans 5:8   1 Peter 3:18

2 Corinthians 5:21

Questions for Group Reflection

1. Are Christians called to silently suffer injustice or to actively preserve and extend justice—or both? Use the following passages to help shore up your answer: Psalm 11:7; Proverbs 31:8–9; Isaiah 1:17; Micah 6:8; Matthew 5:10–12, 38–42; Luke 11:42; 1 Peter 2:19–21.

2. Did you recognize yourself in any of the people you studied in this chapter?

   • *In Jesus*: falsely accused, wrongly convicted, victimized by political maneuvering

   • *In the religious leaders*: violently, murderously angry; blinded by hate to the good in others and the evil in themselves

   • *In Herod*: self-centered, abusive, viewing others as being there for his amusement

   • *In Pilate*: knowing what's right but not having the courage to do it; sacrificing the vulnerable in order to please the crowd

   • *In the crowd*: unthinking, easily swayed, vocal, and vicious

   If you feel comfortable doing so, tell your own story and recount how God has interacted with you. How has your experience changed your perspective?

3. What does Jesus' response teach you about handling those situations in which your rights are trampled for His name? What do you think helped Jesus endure it all (see John 14:2–3; 15:13; Heb. 12:2; 1 Pet. 2:23)?

4. As you draw together for prayer, begin your time by quietly meditating on these words: "Christ also died for sins once for all, the just for the unjust . . ." (1 Pet. 3:18). Silently—or if appropriate, to each other—confess your "unjustness" to the Father. Then bring before Him the injustices in your community, city, state, and nation. And remember to support in prayer those trampled down by the injustice of others.

The Trials of Jesus Christ

Trial	Officiating Authority	Scripture	Accusation	Legality	Type	Result
1	Annas, ex-high priest of the Jews (A.D. 6–15).	John 18:13–23	Trumped-up charges of irreverence to Annas.	ILLEGAL! Held at night. No specific charges. Prejudice. Violence.	Jewish and Religious	Found guilty of irreverence and rushed to Caiaphas.
2	Caiaphas, Annas' son-in-law and high priest (A.D. 18–36), and the Sanhedrin.	Matthew 26:57–68 Mark 14:53–65 John 18:24	Claiming to be the Messiah, the Son of God—blasphemy (worthy of death under Jewish law).	ILLEGAL! Held at night. False witnesses. Prejudice. Violence.	Jewish and Religious	Declared guilty of blasphemy and rushed to the Sanhedrin (Jewish supreme court).
3	The Sanhedrin—seventy ruling men of Israel (their word was needed before Jesus could be taken to Roman officials).	Mark 15:1a Luke 22:66–71	Claiming to be the Son of God—blasphemy.	ILLEGAL! Accusation switched. No witnesses. Improper voting.	Jewish and Religious	Declared guilty of blasphemy and rushed to Roman official, Pilate.
4	Pilate, governor of Judea, who was already in "hot water" with Rome (A.D. 26–36).	Matthew 27:11–14 Mark 15:1b–5 Luke 23:1–7 John 18:28–38	Treason (accusation was changed, since treason was worthy of capital punishment in Rome).	ILLEGAL! Christ was kept under arrest, although He was found innocent. No defense attorney. Violence.	Roman and Civil	Found innocent . . . but rushed to Herod Antipas; mob overruled Pilate.
5	Herod Antipas, governor of Galilee (4 B.C.–A.D. 39).	Luke 23:8–12	No accusation was made.	ILLEGAL! No grounds. Mockery in courtroom. No defense attorney. Violence.	Roman and Civil	Mistreated and mocked; returned to Pilate without decision made by Herod.
6	Pilate (second time).	Matthew 27:15–26 Mark 15:6–15 Luke 23:18–25 John 18:39–19:16	Treason, though not proven (Pilate bargained with the mob, putting Christ on a level with Barabbas, a criminal!)	ILLEGAL! Without proof of guilt, Pilate allowed an innocent man to be condemned.	Roman and Civil	Found innocent, but Pilate "washed his hands" and allowed Him to be crucified.

Chapter 6

THE MAN WHO
MISSED HIS CROSS
Matthew 27:15–26

Imagine sitting on death row, wrestling with all the emotions twisting and straining through your mind as the end draws near. With every appeal for pardon and every stay of execution exhausted, you endure each agonizing minute in hopeless condemnation. There's no way out; your fate is irreversibly sealed.

Suddenly, the muted rhythm of approaching footsteps breaks the silence. A clamor of metal echoes through the chamber as, to your amazement, your cell door swings open. You're ordered to your feet; your shackles are loosed. Through the din of confusion you hear the words: "You are free to go. You've received a pardon. Another will die in your place."

Barabbas experienced just that. Using a bizarre array of circumstances, Matthew paints a magnificent portrait of Christ's substitutionary death on the cross.

As we trace the events described for us in Matthew 27, we'll encounter a stirring scene that gets to the heart of the Gospel: By the unjust death of a righteous man, a world of condemned prisoners is set free.

The Governor

Our scene opens on Pontius Pilate, who is still trying to find a way around putting the innocent Jesus to death.

> Now at the feast the governor was accustomed to release for the people any one prisoner whom they wanted. (Matt. 27:15)

According to Matthew, during Passover it was customary for the governor of Judea to release a prisoner chosen by the crowd (see also Mark 15:6). Though the exact origins of this custom remain a mystery, the tradition played a crucial role in Jesus' fateful journey to the cross. Pilate might have hoped that he could spare Jesus' life this way, but in the end, Jesus' fate was sealed by it.

Let's take a closer look at governor Pilate to gain some insight into the choices he made.

His Power

Pilate ruled as governor, or prefect, of Judea between A.D. 26 and 37.[1] Governors were appointed by the emperor, "had full control in the province," and were "in charge of the army of occupation."[2] Their job was to maintain law and order, to rule on judicial matters (like a judge), and to collect taxes.[3] They determined who would receive the death penalty and who would be pardoned. Interestingly, they also "appointed the high priests and controlled the Temple and its funds."[4]

Although Pilate, as governor, "possessed *imperium*, or the supreme administrative power in the province,"[5] he was still held accountable for the well-being of his jurisdiction. The emperor who appointed Pilate was Tiberius (who ruled from A.D. 14–37), and the person to whom he was accountable was the legate of nearby Syria, "the supreme military commander in the East."[6] This accountability factor would play an important behind-the-scenes role in the condemnation of Jesus.

His Troubled Rule

Based on what we know from the historian Josephus and the philosopher Philo, Pilate was not a big hit with the Jewish people. He wanted Roman rule enforced and recognized, and his attempts to achieve this in Judea were either blunders or deliberately offensive acts. For example, unlike previous governors of that region, when he brought his army in, his soldiers held standards that bore

1. Pilate is sometimes given the title procurator, which means essentially the same as prefect or governor. The Emperor Claudius I (A.D. 41–54) changed the military title of prefect to the civilian title of procurator during his reign, and the writers of his era followed suit. See Helen Bond, "Pontius Pilate," accessed October 26, 2001, available at http://cedar.evans-ville.edu/~ecoleweb/articles/pilate.html.

2. D. H. Wheaton, "Pilate," in *The New Bible Dictionary* (Wheaton, Ill.: Tyndale House Publishers, Inc., 1962).

3. See Bond, "Pontius Pilate."

4. See Wheaton, "Pilate."

5. See Bond, "Pontius Pilate."

6. A. N. Sherwin-White, "Pilate, Pontius," in *The International Standard Bible Encyclopedia*, rev. ed., ed. Geoffrey W. Bromiley (1986; reprint, Grand Rapids, Mich.: William B. Eerdmans Publishing Co., 1987), vol. 3, p. 868.

the emperor's image—a sure affront to Jewish law which eschewed emperor worship. When the people protested, Pilate initially refused to change the banners. But when he saw that the Jewish people were willing to die for their beliefs, he backed down—possibly to avoid a national revolt.[7]

After this, Pilate took a more subtle approach at exalting Roman rule. He brought into his residence at Jerusalem shields that didn't bear an image but instead had an inscription referring to the Caesar Augustus as divine.[8] This caused a row with the Jewish leaders that made it all the way to Tiberius in Rome. In response, Tiberius ordered Pilate to place the shields in a more appropriate setting— a temple dedicated to Augustus in Caesarea.[9]

Later, he tried to build an aqueduct to improve Jerusalem's water supply, but he used temple funds to finance it! The Jewish people violently opposed Pilate's actions—the temple money was God's money, not another deep pocket for a grasping Roman hand. Pilate met their violence with violence of his own, disguising his soldiers as part of the crowd and having them club the protestors. Several of them died in that senseless, vicious attack.[10] It's possible that the incident mentioned in Luke 13:1, regarding "Galileans whose blood Pilate had mixed with their sacrifices," is connected with this incident.

His Death

In his last year in office, A.D. 36, an armed group of Samaritans followed their false-prophet leader up to Mount Gerizim, where they believed Moses' sacred vessels were buried. Pilate blocked their route, and a skirmish ensued. Some of the Samaritan followers were killed in the fight, others were imprisoned, and the leaders were executed. The Samaritan council took their protest to the legate of Syria, who then sent Pilate to Rome to address the matter with

---

7. See H. W. Hoehner, "Pontius Pilate," in *Dictionary of Jesus and the Gospels,* ed. Joel G. Green, Scot McKnight, I. Howard Marshall (Downers Grove, Ill.: InterVarsity Press, 1998).

8. Pilate's main seat of government was at the pagan city of Caesarea; he went to Jerusalem mainly during festivals to maintain order. See Bond, "Pontius Pilate." Caesar Augustus was the first Roman emperor to consider himself a god, going so far as to imprint on coins bearing his image: "Caesar Son of a God." See Encyclopedia Britannica, "Augustus Caesar," accessed October, 2001, available at www.britannica.com.

9. Sherwin-White, "Pilate, Pontius," p. 868.

10. See Hoehner, "Pontius Pilate," pp. 1–2; Sherwin-White, "Pilate, Pontius," p. 868.

Tiberius.[11] Unfortunately for Pilate, Tiberius died before he got to Rome, and he had to deal with the mentally unstable Gaius Caligula. It's possible that Caligula ordered Pilate to commit suicide, though we don't know for certain how or when Pilate died.

With Pilate's history in mind, let's meet the next crucial character in this scene at Jerusalem, where Jesus' fate hangs precariously in the balance.

The Criminal

> At that time they were holding a notorious prisoner, called Barabbas. (Matt. 27:16)

His Name

Barabbas was an Aramaic name that meant either "son of the father" (*bar-abba*) or "son of the teacher" (*bar-rabban*)—which could have meant he was a rabbi's son.[12] If this was the case, it would make his predicament all the more poignant. Here might be an impatient man—one tired of waiting for his father's God to deliver the Jewish people from Roman domination—who took a stand against that oppressive government in his own violent way.

Interestingly, some early Greek manuscripts of Matthew's gospel render his name as Jesus Barabbas, which would present a pointed contrast between the two deliverers: Barabbas, the political revolutionary, and Christ, the true Liberator.[13]

His Crime

Why was this particular prisoner so "notorious," as Matthew calls him?[14] The other gospel writers give us an idea:

> The man named Barabbas had been imprisoned with

11. See Hoehner, "Pontius Pilate," p. 2; Sherwin-White, "Pilate, Pontius," p. 869.

12. See Thomas Rees, "Barabbas," in *The International Standard Bible Encyclopedia*, rev. ed., ed. Geoffrey W. Bromiley (1979; reprint, Grand Rapids, Mich.: William B. Eerdmans Publishing Co., 1988), vol. 1, p. 429.

13. See Rees, "Barabbas," p. 429; and "Barabbas" in *The New Bible Dictionary* (Wheaton, Ill.: Tyndale House Publishers, 1962). This may be why Pilate distinguishes Jesus as "Jesus who is called Christ" (Matt. 27:17, 22).

14. He would have been very well-known in this region. The Greek word for *notorious*, *episemos*, means "'having a distinguishing mark' . . . 'stamped,' 'labeled' . . . 'infamous.'" Gerhard Kittel and Gerhard Friedrich, eds., *Theological Dictionary of the New Testament*, translated and abridged in one volume by Geoffrey W. Bromiley (1985; reprint, Grand Rapids, Mich.: William B. Eerdmans Publishing Co., 1992), p. 1024.

the insurrectionists who had committed murder in the insurrection. (Mark 15:7)

[Barabbas] was the one who had been thrown into prison for an insurrection made in the city, and for murder. (Luke 23:19)

Now Barabbas was a robber. (John 18:40b)

John's description is particularly interesting. The Greek word for *robber, lestes,* was often used in the sense of "bandit"—but not necessarily in the way we would think of it.

> Josephus uses the term for the Zealots, who . . . revolt against Roman rule, perhaps with messianic pretensions. For many Jews the Zealots are patriots rather than bandits, even though they often take what they need from their own people. But Josephus takes the Roman view, for although the Romans execute the Zealots as political offenders (by crucifixion), they contemptuously describe them as bandits. . . .
> . . . Pilate, indeed, lets the people choose between the freedom fighter Barabbas, whose first name was probably Jesus, and Jesus of Nazareth, as though they are both men of the same stamp.[15]

So the infamous and popular Barabbas was languishing under Roman guard, awaiting his fate for revolting against Rome and committing murder in the process.

His Location

Barabbas would most likely have been imprisoned in one of the guardrooms in the Fortress Antonia. This fortress or tower would probably have been Pilate's residence in Jerusalem, called the *Praetorium,* as well as the place where his soldiers were barracked.

So here is the scene: the Jewish leaders took Jesus to Pilate, being careful not to enter the Praetorium because they would be defiled, or unclean, for Passover (see John 18:28). Pilate spoke privately with Jesus inside the Praetorium but talked outside with the religious leaders in an area called The Pavement, where Pilate's

---

15. Kittel and Friedrich, *Theological Dictionary of the New Testament,* pp. 532–33.

judgment seat was located (see 19:13). Barabbas was somewhere inside this fortress, and the crowd was directly outside of it.[16] Barabbas, then, could hear the crowd, but he could not hear Pilate.

Now that we have this rich backdrop in mind, let's watch the larger drama unfold.

The Perilous Decision

> Now at the feast the governor was accustomed to release for the people any one prisoner whom they wanted. At that time they were holding a notorious prisoner, called Barabbas. So when the people gathered together, Pilate said to them, "Whom do you want me to release for you? Barabbas, or Jesus who is called Christ?" For he knew that because of envy they had handed Him over. (Matt. 27:15–18)

Having found Jesus innocent and having had no luck in attempting to pass Him off on Herod (Luke 23:4–7, 11), Pilate was stuck politically. He saw through the religious leaders' motives, yet he did not want to incur their wrath. Humiliated once in front of Emperor Tiberius, Pilate was not going to risk it again.

Then he remembered the Passover custom—maybe this would be his way out! So Pilate put before the people two men—one a murdering, contemptible bandit (in his view), and the other a peaceful rabbi with a penetrating message. One was so blatantly guilty and the other so obviously innocent, what could go wrong?

Everything.

Because a mere bandit in Roman eyes was a freedom fighter in the eyes of the Jewish people.

An Unlikely Advocate

Into the fray came a message from Pilate's wife, which must have unraveled the governor's nerves even further:

> While he was sitting on the judgment seat, his wife sent him a message, saying, "Have nothing to do with that righteous Man; for last night I suffered greatly in a dream because of Him." (Matt. 27:19)

16. See Bastiaan VanElderen, "Praetorium," in *The International Standard Bible Encyclopedia*, rev. ed., ed. Geoffrey W. Bromiley (1986; reprint, Grand Rapids, Mich.: William B. Eerdmans Publishing Co., 1987), vol. 3, p. 929.

The plot thickens with this ominous warning. Clearly, Matthew included this detail as more evidence of Jesus' innocence. The irony, however, is striking. While even a pagan woman remained "open to the voice of God, the Jewish leaders [were] deaf to it!"[17]

Escalating Tension

> But the chief priests and the elders persuaded the crowds to ask for Barabbas and to put Jesus to death. (Matt. 27:20)

The chief priests wanted to release Barabbas? The one who had committed acts of treason? Bent on murdering Jesus, they rallied the crowd to follow their twisted logic, and the people didn't seem to put up much resistance to their plan:

> The governor said to them, "Which of the two do you want me to release for you?" And they said, "Barabbas." Pilate said to them, "Then what shall I do with Jesus who is called Christ?" They all said, "Crucify Him!" And he said, "Why, what evil has He done?" But they kept shouting all the more, saying, "Crucify Him!" (vv. 21–23)

By now, all of Jerusalem must have been embroiled in this drama. But picture it for a moment from Barabbas' perspective. Most likely, here is what he heard:

> "Barabbas . . . crucify him! Crucify him!" (from vv. 21 and 23)

> "Not this Man, but Barabbas. . . . Away with him, away with him, crucify him! . . . We have no king but Caesar!" (John 18:40; 19:15)

It must have terrified him. The people he fought for had turned against him! They would crucify him and bow to Rome! There would be no deliverance for the deliverer.

He could not have known, however, that his destiny had been divinely enjoined to that of Jesus.

---

17. As quoted by Leon Morris in *The Gospel according to Matthew* (Grand Rapids, Mich.: William B. Eerdmans Publishing Co., 1992), p. 704, fn. 38.

A Substitution Made

> When Pilate saw that he was accomplishing nothing, but rather that a riot was starting, he took water and washed his hands in front of the crowd, saying, "I am innocent of this Man's blood; see to that yourselves." And all the people said, "His blood shall be on us and on our children!" Then he released Barabbas for them; but after having Jesus scourged, he handed Him over to be crucified. (Matt. 27:24–26)

A riot—just what Pilate wanted to avoid, especially with so many Jews in Jerusalem for their Passover festival. From his perspective, it would only mean more trouble with these troublesome people, more embarrassment with Tiberius.[18] So Pilate abdicated his responsibility to uphold justice by letting the crowd have their way.

Barabbas, meanwhile, came stumbling and blinking out into the sunlight. Though he should have been condemned, he was released. The freedom fighter had his freedom, but through no fight of his own. Someone else would be on that cross—fighting sin and death for him—and He would win the victory through laying down His arms.

And the crowd? They thought that their greatest enemy was Rome, not the sin in their own hearts that kept them bound and oppressed, marring every day of their lives. So they released their hero, Barabbas (of whom we hear nothing more after he slipped into the crowds), and sentenced to death the Giver of life. As William Barclay so eloquently observes, "They preferred the man of violence to the man of love."[19]

We cannot help but ask ourselves now, which man do we prefer?

18. John illuminates the kind of pressure Jewish religious leaders were putting on Pilate. In John 19:12, they tell the troubled governor: "If you release this Man, you are no friend of Caesar." This statement "hints at an investigation on a charge of *maiestas minuta*—neglect of the security of the state." Sherwin-White, "Pilate, Pontius," p. 868.

19. William Barclay, *The Gospel of Matthew*, rev. ed., The Daily Study Bible Series (Philadelphia, Pa.: Westminster Press, 1975), vol. 2, p. 362.

Living Insights

Shoulders hunched, a man plods through life, straining with every step to carry the great burden on his back. It has been his night-and-day companion. Not once has he known relief from its merciless weight.

The man's name is Christian, the central character in John Bunyan's classic allegory _The Pilgrim's Progress_. In one moving scene, Christian finds the path to salvation. Up the hill he staggers until he reaches the peak. There he sees a wooden cross and, just below it, an empty sepulchre. As he nears the cross, a miracle happens. The straps binding the massive weight to his shoulders loosen, and his load tumbles away into the tomb's waiting mouth, never to be seen again.

A delicious feeling of lightness buoys Christian's body, and joyous tears of relief stream down his face. Three Shining Ones then approach him. The first announces, "Thy sins be forgiven thee"; the second strips away his rags and dresses him in splendid clothes; the third hands him a sealed scroll, which he is to present when he enters the Celestial City. [20]

Overwhelmed by his new freedom, Christian sings:

> "Thus far did I come laden with my sin;
> Nor could aught ease the grief that I was in,
> Till I came hither: what a place is this!
> Must here be the beginning of my bliss?
> Must here the burden fall from off my back?
> Must here the strings that bound it to me crack?
> Blest cross! blest sepulchre! blest rather be
> The Man that was there put to shame for me!"

A song of a soul set free. Are you singing it today? [21]

---

20. John Bunyan, _The Pilgrim's Progress_ (Old Tappan, N.J.: Fleming H. Revell Co, Spire Books, 1977), p. 39.

21. Bunyan, _The Pilgrim's Progress_, p. 40.

Questions for Group Reflection

1. What do Pilate's and Barabbas' histories tell you about God's sovereignty? Does the Lord's sovereignty excuse our choices and actions—in other words, does the end justify the means? What light does Romans 8:28 shed on these issues?

2. Why do you suppose we so often prefer violence to love? What are the challenges love offers us that violence does not? What challenges does violence offer us that love does not?

3. Because of Christ, Barabbas could walk free. He was no longer under condemnation, no longer in the deep shadow of death. By Christ dying in his place, he got his life back. How real to you is Christ's substitution for you on the cross?

4. This scene from the Gospels is humbling, isn't it? As you come together in quietness now to pray, draw your hearts close to God's love: "For God so loved the world, that He gave His only begotten Son . . . that the world might be saved by Him" (John 3:16a, 17b); "How wide and long and high and deep is the love of Christ" (Eph. 3:18 NIV). Thank the Lord for His great love for you. Express to Him what it means to you that He was willing to give up His life so that you may have true, everlasting life.

Chapter 7

THE WAY OF THE CROSS
Selected Scripture

Reflecting on the beloved hymn "The Old Rugged Cross," John Fischer, in his book *On a Hill Too Far Away*, makes some poignant observations about the nature of the cross:

> How can you have a love affair with a cross? How can you cherish an apparatus of execution? How could anyone want to cling to a hard, splintery beam of wood? How is it possible to find beauty in its bloodstreamed grains? It seems awkward to use such warm, friendly terms when speaking of a death device, but this is merely one more inexplicable aspect of the cross. Sooner or later, if you have found forgiveness there, this cut and planed trunk of a tree actually becomes something cherished.[1]

Believers the world over cherish the old rugged cross. For it was on the cross that the Savior of the world raised His bloodstained head and asked the Judge of the universe not for vengeance or even for justice, but for mercy on those who crucified Him. His death delivered a peace offering to a holy God on our behalf. Through the Cross, humanity received a second chance. And an eagerly awaiting Father received His Son.

As we shall see, crucifixion was the most cruel way for our Lord to die . . . but by His agonizing death, He made a way for us to really live!

The Crucifixion

Before looking in-depth at John's account of Jesus' death, let's understand the biblical perspective on the Crucifixion and get the setting firm in our minds.

This chapter has been adapted from the chapter "Delivered Up to Be Crucified," in the Bible study guide *The Majesty of God's Son*, by Jason Shepherd, from the Bible-teaching ministry of Charles R. Swindoll (Anaheim, Calif.: Charles R. Swindoll, Inc., 1999).

1. John Fischer, *On a Hill Too Far Away: Putting the Cross Back into the Center of Our Lives* (Minneapolis, Minn.: Bethany House Publishers, 2001), p. 168.

A Predetermined Plan

Some people have the false impression that Jesus fell victim to an insidious plot that left Him little more than a pitiful martyr whose plans suddenly and unexpectedly terminated at the cross. But this was not the case at all. His death had been carefully predicted in the Scriptures.

As Peter testified, Christ's sacrificial death took place as part of God's predetermined plan:

> "Men of Israel, listen to these words: Jesus the Nazarene, a man attested to you by God with miracles and wonders and signs which God performed through Him in your midst, just as you yourselves know—this Man, *delivered over by the predetermined plan and foreknowledge of God*, you nailed to a cross by the hands of godless men and put Him to death." (Acts 2:22–23, emphasis added)

Later in Acts 3:18, Peter proclaimed that this predetermined plan was "announced beforehand by the mouth of all the prophets." In this study we look at several of these prophecies, such as Isaiah 53 and Psalm 22. Isaiah described the misery, torture, and intense pain of God's Servant, the Lord God's planning of His Servant's death, and His dying alongside sinners. Psalm 22 foretold Christ's suffering and death with amazing accuracy and detail: hands and feet pierced, bones pulled out of joint, lots cast for the division of clothing, innocence scorned and mocked.

From all of Scripture, it's clear that Christ was not murdered in an abrupt act of passion; His death was part of God's eternal plan of redemption.

Time and Place

After Pilate's verdict, the governor delivered Jesus over to be scourged and crucified (John 19:16; Mark 15:15). This most likely occurred between 7:30 a.m. and 8:00 a.m.

The actual sentencing of Jesus took place at the judgment seat just outside the Praetorium in the Fortress Antonia near Herod's temple, as John tells us:

> Therefore when Pilate heard these words, he brought Jesus out, and sat down on the judgment

seat at a place called The Pavement, but in Hebrew, Gabbatha. (John 19:13)

Roman soldiers customarily stayed in this fortress to maintain law and order during Jewish feasts, such as Passover. No doubt they looked down from their windows as Pilate presented Jesus to the people. For them, this was great sport.

Christ's Suffering

Following Pilate's verdict, the Romans subjected Jesus to cruel and inhumane torture, finally nailing Him to the cross. As disturbing as these scenes are, it is necessary to walk with Him through these agonized hours in order to appreciate in full the depth of His love for us.

The Scourging

Although completely unwarranted and unnecessary—yet in keeping with Roman custom[2]—Pilate ordered that Jesus be scourged (Matt. 27:26; Mark 15:15). Two kinds of scourging were administered in Jesus' day: Jewish and Roman. Jewish law specified that the victim could not receive more than forty lashes (Deut. 25:1–3). Roman law, however, was not so humane. A man trained in torture, called a *lictor,* administered the scourging:

> Crucifixion was prefaced by scourging, either on the way to the cross or before the victim began the trip to the cross. Tied to a post, the condemned person would be beaten with the flagellum: a leather whip with metal knotted into its thongs. This whipping bloodied the victim's back, leaving strips of flesh hanging from the wounds. By weakening the victim's constitution, it would mercifully shorten the time it would take the condemned person to die on the cross.[3]

In a stirring article that appeared in an issue of *The Journal of*

2. See David W. Wead, "Scourge," in *The International Standard Bible Encyclopedia,* rev. ed., ed. Geoffrey W. Bromiley (Grand Rapids, Mich.: William B. Eerdmans Publishing Co., 1988), vol. 4, p. 359. Wead adds, "On some occasions these beatings were so severe that bones and organs were left exposed."

3. Craig S. Keener, *The IVP Bible Background Commentary on the New Testament* (Downers Grove, Ill.: InterVarsity Press, 1993), p. 126.

the American Medical Association, a team of medical and theological professionals describes this tortuous event in vivid detail:

> As the Roman soldiers repeatedly struck the victim's back with full force, the iron balls would cause deep contusions, and the leather thongs and sheep bones would cut into the skin and subcutaneous tissues. Then, as the flogging continued, the lacerations would tear into the underlying skeletal muscles and produce quivering ribbons of bleeding flesh. Pain and blood loss generally set the stage for circulatory shock. The extent of blood loss may well have determined how long the victim would survive on the cross. . . .
>
> The severe scourging, with its intense pain and appreciable blood loss, most probably left Jesus in a preshock state. Moreover, hematidrosis had rendered his skin particularly tender. The physical and mental abuse meted out by the Jews and the Romans, as well as the lack of food, water, and sleep, also contributed to his generally weakened state. Therefore, even before the actual crucifixion, Jesus' physical condition was at least serious and possibly critical.[4]

As if pain from intense physical torture were not enough, Jesus also endured the emotional pain of cruel humiliation.

The Robe

After the nearly fatal scourging, the soldiers circled like vultures around Christ's dying body, moving in to pick at the remains with biting words and shameful taunts:

> Then the soldiers of the governor took Jesus into the Praetorium and gathered the whole Roman cohort around Him. They stripped Him and put a scarlet robe on Him. (Matt. 27:27–28)

This was not the kind of long, flowing robe commonly seen in Easter pageants. Rather, the Greek word for *robe* here, *chlamus*,

4. William D. Edwards, M.D., Wesley J. Gabel, M.Div., and Floyd E. Hosmer, M.S., A.M.I., "On the Physical Death of Jesus Christ," in JAMA: *The Journal of the American Medical Association* 255, no. 11 (March 21, 1986), pp. 1457–58.

suggests a short cloak worn over the shoulders. His body exposed from the waist down, Jesus became the object of vulgar remarks which the gospel writers understandably chose to omit from the record.

The Crown

The soldiers continued their cruelty by giving this King a "crown":

> And after twisting together a crown of thorns, they put it on His head, and a reed in His right hand; and they knelt down before Him and mocked Him, saying, "Hail, King of the Jews!" They spat on Him, and took the reed and began to beat Him on the head. After they had mocked Him, they took the scarlet robe off Him and put His own garments back on Him, and led Him away to crucify Him. (vv. 29–31)

Mocking, jeering, abusing—it's as if each soldier tried to top the other's joke. They took turns spitting on Jesus . . . cursing His name . . . beating Him with the reed. Jesus, at whose name every knee will someday bow. Jesus, before whom every tongue will someday confess that He is Lord. This Jesus stood humiliated, beaten, bloodied and torn, absorbing every blow with a silent, patient dignity (see 1 Pet. 2:23).

The Journey to the Cross

After dressing Jesus, the soldiers followed their usual course with criminals: such a victim was surrounded by four Roman soldiers and led by a centurion, all the while struggling to carry the six-foot crossbeam that would later be attached to the larger, vertical post of the cross. And so it was with Jesus. After the scourging and beating, however, He was too weak to carry the beam Himself. Matthew tells us that Simon of Cyrene was pressed into service to help Him (Matt. 27:32).

Once at the site, a placard was placed above Jesus' head that read, "Jesus the Nazarene, the King of the Jews," not only in Hebrew but also in Latin and Greek (John 19:19–20). The chief priests objected to the wording:

> The chief priests of the Jews were saying to Pilate, "Do not write, 'The King of the Jews'; but that He said, 'I am King of the Jews.'" Pilate answered, "What I have written I have written." (John 19:21–22)

Death on a Cross

The barbaric form of capital punishment known as *crucifixion* originated with the Persians, who possibly learned it from the Assyrian practice of impaling criminals on sharpened beams. [5] In crucifixion, death came slowly and painfully—from exposure, exhaustion, and finally suffocation. And to ensure the greatest amount of humiliation, it was always done in plain view of a watching public. Jim Bishop, in his book *The Day Christ Died*, conveys the horror of this kind of death:

> The executioner laid the crossbeam behind Jesus and brought him to the ground quickly by grasping his arm and pulling him backward. As soon as Jesus fell, the beam was fitted under the back of his neck and, on each side, soldiers quickly knelt on the inside of his elbows. . . . The thorns pressed against his torn scalp.
>
> . . . With his right hand, the executioner probed the wrist of Jesus to find the little hollow spot. When he found it, he took one of the square-cut iron nails . . . raised the hammer over the nail head and brought it down with force. . . .
>
> Two soldiers grabbed each side of the crossbeam and lifted. As they pulled up, they dragged Jesus by the wrists. With every breath, he groaned. When the soldiers reached the upright, the four of them began to lift the crossbeam higher until the feet of Jesus were off the ground. The body must have writhed with pain. . . .
>
> When the crossbeam was set firmly, the executioner . . . knelt before the cross. Two soldiers hurried to help, and each one took hold of a leg at the calf. The ritual was to nail the right foot over the left, and this was probably the most difficult part of the work. If the feet were pulled downward, and nailed too close to the foot of the cross, the prisoner always died quickly. Over the years, the Romans

---

5. See "Crucifixion as a Death Penalty: A Brief History," accessed on October 31, 2001, available at http://www.mindspring.com/~stjoseph/crucifix.html.

learned to push the feet upward on the cross, so that the condemned man could lean on the nails and stretch himself upward [to breathe].[6]

Each movement cut deeper into the bone and tendons and raw muscle. Fever inevitably set in, inflaming the wounds and creating an insatiable thirst. Waves of hallucinations caused the victim to drift in and out of consciousness. And in time, flies and other insects found their way to the open wounds.

By this time, Jesus knew He had accomplished everything His Father had sent Him to do. And to fulfill one final Scripture, He said:

> "I am thirsty." A jar full of sour wine was standing there; so they put a sponge full of the sour wine upon a branch of hyssop and brought it up to His mouth. (John 19:28b–29; see also Ps. 69:3, 21)

With a final effort, Jesus exclaimed, *"Tetelestai"*—"It is finished!" His saving work was done, and now He could rest. Quietly, peacefully, He bowed His head and then died.

The next verses of this passage represent John's eyewitness account of what was done with the Lord's body. Because Jewish law demanded that the dead be buried before sunset, the Romans would usually expedite the process by breaking the victim's legs (vv. 31–32). But when the soldiers came to Jesus, they saw that He was already dead, so they didn't break His legs (v. 33). But in one last brutal act, a soldier stabbed Him in the side, and water mixed with blood streamed out (v. 34).[7]

As the darkness lifted from the sky (see Matt. 27:45; Mark 15:33; Luke 23:44), the crowd slowly dispersed. Jesus was dead. His blood had been shed, His body broken . . . just as He had predicted. It was for the world He loved . . . including you and me. The writer of Hebrews tells us, "By this will we have been sanctified through the offering of the body of Jesus Christ once for all" (Heb. 10:10).

---

6. Jim Bishop, *The Day Christ Died* (1957, Harper and Brothers; reprint, New York, N.Y.: Harper and Row, 1977), pp. 311–12.

7. One sign of death is the quick separation of dark red corpuscles from the thin, whitish serum of the blood, here called "water" (v. 34). Normally, the dead don't bleed. But after death, the right auricle of the human heart fills with blood, and the membrane surrounding the heart, the pericardium, holds the watery serum. Jesus' heart must have been punctured with the Roman spear, causing both fluids to flow from His side.

The work was accomplished. A way of peace was forged.

That's why we cherish the old rugged cross . . . not because of its horror that grieves us, but because of its triumphant power that transforms us!

> For the word of the cross is foolishness to those
> who are perishing, but to us who are being saved it
> is the power of God. (1 Cor. 1:18)

 Living Insights

"It is finished!" With these words, the Good Shepherd laid down His life for His sheep. The Light of the World closed His eyes, pillowed His head on His Father's chest, and rested from His work. What indescribable love hung on a cross and died to bring sinful human beings into the wonders of heaven!

Thoughtfully and prayerfully, read the verses that describe Jesus' crucifixion. Allow the spirit of God to speak to you. As you do, remember: The work is finished. The sinless One took on our sins, paid for our crimes, hung in our place. He died that we might live. Spend some time in prayer, thanking Him, asking Him to let this reality sink more deeply into your heart, telling Him how much you love Him. There is no other way to heaven for us but through the ordeal of the Cross. Remember that. And remember the One who considered it a victory for you![8]

 Questions for Group Reflection

These scenes of Jesus' Crucifixion—His being mocked, cruelly abused, nailed to and hanging on a cross, stabbed—are painful to look at and think about. Yet that's just what the Lord wants us to do. Each of the gospel writers slows down his account here, recording Jesus' last journey in aching detail.

---

8. This Living Insight has been adapted from the Bible study guide *Exalting Christ . . . the Lamb of God: A Study of John 15–21*, rev. ed., Living Insight by Wendy Peterson, from the Bible-teaching ministry of Charles R. Swindoll (Anaheim, Calif.: Insight for Living, 2000), pp. 93–94.

1. What does this somber, awesome event tell you about the nature of God? Which scenes speak to you most?

2. What does this event tell you about human nature (read also John 19:23–27)?

3. What does it tell you about God's love?

4. The Cross is so immense that it's hard to get our minds and hearts around it, isn't it? Sometimes the best we can do is bring our fragmented thoughts, heavy hearts, and stumbling words to the Lord, who faced death so that we might live. So gather around Jesus, the Lamb of God, and express to Him all that's in your heart.

Chapter 8

"FATHER, FORGIVE THEM"
Luke 23:33–34

At the beginning of World War II, enemy bombs destroyed England's magnificent Coventry Cathedral, leaving the beloved place of worship in ruins. Only a charred cross and part of one wall were still visible. Years later, tourists visiting the site happened upon an inscription carved on the wall that read simply: "Father, forgive."[1]

Author Warren Wiersbe makes some observations about this astonishing inscription:

> Father, forgive! This was the prayer of an anguished people who were watching their buildings being destroyed and their loved ones and friends being maimed and killed. Father, forgive! When you look at the ruins of the old cathedral, you can see a monument to man's selfishness and sin, but you can also see a memorial to the grace of God that enables Christians to pray for their enemies. "Father, forgive!"[2]

Jesus' Seven Last Sayings

History abounds with famous last words. However, of all the most significant and profound final statements on record, none compares to the remarkable last sayings of Christ from the cross. These sayings are summarized in a chart at the end of this chapter.

"Father, Forgive Them"

All four gospel writers briefly describe the place where Jesus' death occurred. They call it *Golgotha*, Hebrew for "the Skull," or "The Place of the Skull." Luke, however, moves quickly from detailing the place of Jesus' death to giving an account of what He said in the final moments of His life:

When they came to the place called The Skull, there

---

1. See Warren W. Wiersbe, *The Cross of Jesus: What His Words from Calvary Mean for Us* (Grand Rapids, Mich.: Baker Book House, 1997), p. 51.

2. Wiersbe, *The Cross of Jesus*, p. 51.

they crucified Him and the criminals, one on the
right and the other on the left. But Jesus was saying,
"Father, forgive them; for they do not know what
they are doing." (Luke 23:33–34a)

It's hard to believe that anyone in Jesus' situation could speak
such gracious words. When we've been severely wronged by others,
it's difficult to offer forgiveness. Instead, we tend to harbor regret,
bitterness, and anger towards those who have hurt us deeply.

Let's explore the theological and spiritual significance of Jesus'
words to see how He was able to have such a loving response to
His enemies.

His Words Fulfill Prophecy

Jesus' prayerful request that His Father forgive His accusers was
predicted much earlier. Almost eight hundred years before Christ's
birth, the prophet Isaiah wrote these words:

Therefore, I will allot Him a portion with the great,
And He will divide the booty with the strong;
Because He poured out Himself to death,
And was numbered with the transgressors;
Yet He Himself bore the sin of many,
And *interceded for the transgressors*.
(Isa. 53:12, emphasis added)

The pure, spotless Lamb of God, praying for sinful people! As
He was being tested in the crucible of intense suffering and anguish,
Jesus prayed not for Himself, but for the enemies of righteousness,
just as Isaiah had predicted.

Again, Warren Wiersbe makes some helpful observations:

When we're suffering, most of us intercede for ourselves and not for others; Jesus forgot himself and
thought of others. For God to forgive their sins was
far more important than for God to remove his own
Son's sufferings. Jesus had willingly yielded himself
to die on the cross, so that important matter was
already settled, but he wanted everybody to know
that he forgave them for the way they treated him.[3]

3. Wiersbe, *The Cross of Jesus*, p. 54.

His Words Were Repeated

Most people probably assume Jesus spoke these words only once as He was being crucified. But the tense of the verb suggests that He prayed them repeatedly during the ordeal. In other words, "Jesus kept on saying" is a more literal translation. Each time He suffered a wrong or injustice, He prayed, "Father, forgive them; for they do not know what they are doing."

As the soldiers placed Him on the cross, they heard, "Father, forgive them; for they do not know what they are doing." When they lifted Him into place above the ground, He prayed, "Father, forgive them; for they do not know what they are doing." Each time people taunted Him and mocked Him as He hung in agony on the cross, He quietly interceded, "Father, forgive them; for they do not know what they are doing." With each cruel act, Jesus prayed for the forgiveness of His executors. What amazing, unselfish love!

Now that we've seen a wider view of the context, let's examine the elements of Christ's prayer more closely.

A Closer Look at Christ's Prayer

> "Father, forgive them; for they do not know what they are doing." (Luke 23:34a)

To Whom Christ Prayed

Jesus appealed to His Father. Up to this time, Christ Himself granted forgiveness to sinners in response to their faith in Him (Matt. 9:1–6; Mark 2:1–5, 9–11; Luke 8:44–48). So why the appeal here to the Father?

During His ministry, Jesus clearly demonstrated that He was the Messiah by performing miracles, healing physical afflictions, and forgiving sins. In response to the Pharisees' indignant reaction to His healing *and* forgiving a young paralytic, Jesus said:

> "Why are you thinking evil in your hearts? Which is easier, to say, 'Your sins are forgiven,' or to say, 'Get up, and walk'? But so that you may know that the Son of Man has authority on earth to forgive sins"—then He said to the paralytic, "Get up, pick up your bed and go home." (Matt. 9:4b–6)

While on earth, Jesus had the authority to forgive sins. But on the cross, He fulfilled a new role—our substitute for sin. He willingly submitted to God the Father and deferred to Him the authority to forgive sins.

For What Christ Prayed

"Father, forgive them." (Luke 23:34a)

What a truly amazing request! Imagine having someone drive stakes into your hands and feet and raise you in humiliation onto a rough, splintery cross. Would you feel like praying for them? It's unthinkable! Human nature calls for revenge and retaliation at such terrible injustice. But Jesus didn't have that response. He modeled what He had taught His people by lovingly interceding on behalf of His enemies.

We may be tempted to say, "Well, of course He was able to do that! After all, He is the Son of God." But let's compare Jesus' words with those of Stephen before his own violent death, recorded by Luke in Acts 7:

> When they had driven him out of the city, they began stoning him; and the witnesses laid aside their robes at the feet of a young man named Saul. They went on stoning Stephen . . . Then falling on his knees, he cried out with a loud voice, "Lord, do not hold this sin against them!" Having said this, he fell asleep. (vv. 58–60)

Stephen was able to forgive those who were stoning him to death. He responded to their hate with God's love, echoing the words of Jesus. Although we may not *feel* like reacting graciously when people offend us, Stephen's example shows that we are empowered to do so by the Holy Spirit, even when our lives are at stake. The love of Christ allows us to forgive even those we consider unforgivable.

The remarkable prayers of Jesus and Stephen also demonstrate clearly that forgiveness is a *choice*. Once we choose to throw off our feelings of bitterness and anger, we are free to enjoy the healing and restoration that come from offering Christ's forgiveness to others. Because of the cross, not only can we be forgiven, but we can also be *forgiving*!

For Whom Christ Prayed

As the Roman soldiers carried out their orders for Jesus' execution, He prayed for His Father to forgive them. But certainly Jesus meant to include the hostile Jewish religious leaders and the crowd who called for Him to be crucified (Luke 23:21). Luke explicitly implicated the Pharisees in His record of Paul's sermon in Acts 13:

> "Brethren, sons of Abraham's family, and those among you who fear God, to us the message of this salvation has been sent. For those who live in Jerusalem, and their rulers, recognizing neither Him nor the utterances of the prophets which are read every Sabbath, fulfilled these by condemning Him. And though they found no ground for putting Him to death, they asked Pilate that He be executed." (vv. 26–28)

Even the apostle Paul held the Jewish leaders and the people they influenced answerable for the Messiah's death. Yet Christ asked His Father to forgive even them—the ones who should have recognized most clearly that He was the Son of God.

The Reason Christ Prayed

Jesus came to save sinners, not condemn them. So He asked His Father to forgive His enemies because of their ignorance. This may be understandable given the pagan lifestyle of the Romans, but what about the Jewish people and their leaders? They surely understood the gravity of putting an innocent man to death. How could they be forgiven because of their ignorance? Raymond Brown offers some insight:

> No matter how much the evil was plotted, the perpetrators can always be said not to have known (that is, appreciated God's goodness or plan) or else they would not have acted as they did. In opposing Jesus' followers to the point of stoning them, a Paul who was allied with the chief priests said: "I myself was convinced that it was necessary *to do* many *things* against the name of Jesus the Nazorean" (Acts 26:9). Yet surely Luke would judge that Paul did not know what he was doing. . . . If there were those who did not know because they had not been told, there

were also those who did not know because, although they had been told, they did not grasp.[4]

Some were ignorant because they had not heard. Others did not know because, having heard, they refused to listen (see Acts 3:13–17; 7:51–53). Regardless of the reason, Jesus asked His Father to forgive them.

The Answer

What did Christ's prayer accomplish? God the Father answered His Son's prayer by having mercy on sinners. Through Jesus' death on the cross, God accomplished His plan of forgiveness for the sins of the whole world. Paul explains the significance of Christ's sacrifice in the book of Colossians:

> When you were dead in your transgressions and the uncircumcision of your flesh, He made you alive together with Him, having forgiven us all our transgressions, having canceled out the certificate of debt consisting of decrees against us, which was hostile to us; and He has taken it out of the way, having nailed it to the cross. (2:13–14)

God continues to seek lost sinners and to offer them grace and forgiveness through His Son, Jesus Christ. The Lord wants His children to model that grace by lovingly forgiving others:

> So, as those who have been chosen of God, holy and beloved, put on a heart of compassion, kindness, humility, gentleness and patience; bearing with one another, and forgiving each other, whoever has a complaint against anyone; just as the Lord forgave you, so also should you. (Col. 3:12–13)

We can demonstrate God's love by showing compassion and kindness—even to those who don't deserve it! That's true forgiveness. That's *grace*!

---

4. Raymond E. Brown, *The Death of the Messiah: From Gethsemane to the Grave* (New York, N.Y.: Doubleday, 1994), vol. 2, p. 973.

Did you know that Jericho is an oasis? That's right. If you toured Israel, you would board a bus somewhere in Jerusalem and head down the steep, winding slopes of the Judean Hills cradling the ancient city. You'd be struck at once by the dry, treeless terrain just outside the city limits. You would actually see the intense heat rising from the jagged hillsides cracked by the relentless desert sun. Then you'd see Jericho down below through the tinted bus window. A beautiful, palm-lined city, sparkling in the sunlight. As you approached, the dry earth would give way to lush, tree-lined gardens and walkways spotted with fruit groves and flower beds . . . an oasis in the desert.

What made the difference? Water! Flowing in abundant supply in Jericho. The effects of the refreshing streams of water can be seen everywhere. For centuries on end, the cool, flowing waters of Jericho have refreshed and relieved the weariest travelers.

What a wonderful picture of the body of Christ! Ray Pritchard notes:

> I think it enormously significant that the first word from the cross is a word of forgiveness. These words teach us that Jesus came to establish a religion of forgiveness. *He is at heart a man of forgiveness.* He came into this world to establish a church that would be an oasis of forgiveness. And bring to the world a race of forgiving men and women.[5]

Is your church an oasis of forgiveness? Can weary, broken sinners find relief and mercy *within its walls*? What about the divorced? The recovering addict? The ex-convict? The pregnant teen?

How about your home? Do you foster a safe, gentle environment where grace runs freely and wrongs are forgiven? Or do grudges abound? Are destructive patterns of flaring tempers and buried anger evident in your family?

Jesus' prayer in Luke 23 shows us a better way to live and to love. We can start by embracing His forgiveness for us and for our

---

5. Ray Pritchard, *The Shadow of the Cross: The Deeper Meaning of Calvary* (Nashville, Tenn.: Broadman & Holman Publishers, 2001), p. 17.

sins. And we can continually offer Him a sacrifice of thanksgiving for what He's done for us.

But then that grace must flow freely to others, like the waters of Jericho, offering much-needed refreshment to people literally dying of spiritual thirst.

Are you harboring an unforgiving spirit toward someone today? Have you been hurt so deeply that you can't imagine any way in the world to forgive the person who wronged you?

Then you're invited to spend some time at the foot of the cross. Reflect on Jesus' words: "Father, forgive them; for they do not know what they are doing." Ask the Lord to help you release your own anger and bitterness and to transform them into gushing streams of forgiveness and love.

After all, that's exactly what He did for you!

 Questions for Group Reflection

1. What have you learned about forgiveness from your study of Christ's words from the cross?

2. Times of suffering often tend to make us self-focused rather than others-focused. How did Jesus model love for others while on the cross? What steps can we take to be more loving and selfless, even during difficult times in our lives?

3. Is there anyone in your life toward whom you have been harboring resentment or unforgiveness? If so, who? What situation caused the problem? What steps can you take to offer forgiveness to this person and obtain healing from God?

4. Is there anyone in your life from whom you need to ask forgiveness for a wrong you may have done them, whether intentionally or unintentionally? If so, plan a specific time when you can contact or meet with the person to talk things out, ask for forgiveness, and seek to restore your relationship.

5. Take some time to pray together about this area of forgiveness. You may wish to pray in groups of two so you can pray more specifically for each other's needs.

JESUS' FINAL SAYINGS FROM THE CROSS

First Three Sayings	Last Four Sayings
"Father, forgive them; for they do not know what they are doing." *Luke 23:34a* "Today you shall be with Me in Paradise." *Luke 23:43* "Woman, behold, your son . . ." *John 19:26–27*	"My God, My God, why have You forsaken Me?" *Matthew 27:46* "I am thirsty" *John 19:28* "It is finished!" *John 19:30* "Father, into Your hands I commit My spirit." *Luke 23:46*
Uttered in daylight	Uttered in darkness
Emphasis on Jesus' compassion	Emphasis on Jesus' suffering
Spoken to people	Spoken to His Father
Related to other people: enemies, criminals, and family members	Related to Himself in anguish and triumph

Chapter 9

"TODAY YOU SHALL BE WITH ME"

Luke 23:42–43

Hell seemed to have broken its chains and run loose that day. Jesus, stripped naked, beaten beyond recognition, bleeding from His wounds, hung on a cross between two convicted murderers. Yet the Son of Love, relentless in His supreme mission despite His desperate agony, sought a lost sinner, found him, and promised him paradise.

In his book *Death on a Friday Afternoon*, Richard John Neuhaus notes:

> [T]here is something poignant, even pathetic, in this story. Here is the epicenter of the great drama of cosmic salvation. In Jesus the Christ, God has become man; as true man he lives a life in unqualified responsiveness to the Father; on the cross he does what has never been done before—he makes a perfect offering of love without blemish. And what does he have to show for it? The plan was for the salvation of the world, but after all this he returns to his heavenly home with the pathetic prize of one repentant thief.[1]

Yet, in this "pathetic prize," the paradox of the cross comes into view. The blameless Savior-King died a criminal's death so nameless sinners like you and me could enter the kingdom of God.

Let's listen in on the remarkable dialogue between two criminals and Christ as eternal life and eternal death literally hung in the balance.

A Life-and-Death Dialogue

> One of the criminals who were hanged there was hurling abuse at Him, saying, "Are You not the Christ?

---

1. Richard John Neuhaus, *Death on a Friday Afternoon: Meditations on the Last Words of Jesus from the Cross* (New York, N.Y.: Basic Books, 2000), p. 42.

Save Yourself and us!" But the other answered, and rebuking him said, "Do you not even fear God, since you are under the same sentence of condemnation? And we indeed are suffering justly, for we are receiving what we deserve for our deeds; but this man has done nothing wrong." And he was saying, "Jesus, remember me when You come in Your kingdom!" And He said to him, "Truly I say to you, today you shall be with Me in Paradise." (Luke 23:39–43)

According to Luke, Jesus died between two criminals. The word Luke uses, however, suggests they were more than just petty thieves. Rather, they were evildoers—men who had lived lawless lives. It's possible they were associated with a covert scheme devised to overthrow the Roman government. And it's possible that these men are the ones referred to in Mark 15:7 as the "insurrectionists" imprisoned with Barabbas. According to William Barclay:

It was of set and deliberate purpose that the authorities crucified Jesus between two known criminals. It was deliberately so staged to humiliate Jesus in front of the crowd and to rank him with robbers.[2]

Matthew and Mark tell us in their gospels that both men "hurled insults" at Jesus, joining the mocking crowd in their slanderous taunts. Here's how Matthew describes the scene:

The robbers who had been crucified with Him were also insulting Him with the same words. (Matt. 27:44)

The insults heaped on Jesus were nothing less than blasphemy as these men and others mocked Him and slandered His name. Ironically, blasphemy was the charge brought by the high priest against Jesus before dragging Him to Pilate (Mark 14:62–64). But His accusers were the ones who were guilty of this charge, not Jesus!

Remarkably, Jesus remained silent with each successive insult. Dying and bleeding, He quietly endured not only intense physical suffering, but cruel emotional and verbal abuse as well.

Then something astonishing occurred—one of the dying criminals had a change of heart.

2. William Barclay, *The Gospel of Luke*, rev. ed., The Daily Study Bible Series (Philadelphia, Pa.: Westminster Press, 1975), p. 286.

One Thief's Change of Heart

> But the other answered, and rebuking him said, "Do you not even fear God, since you are under the same sentence of condemnation? And we indeed are suffering justly, for we are receiving what we deserve for our deeds; but this man has done nothing wrong." And he was saying, "Jesus, remember me when You come in Your kingdom!" (Luke 23:40–42).

What made the difference? What could possibly have transformed this dying criminal's slanderous insults into a full confession of faith? Most scholars agree on three main catalysts that may have caused such a radical change in this man's heart.

The Inscription

Perhaps what caused the criminal to believe was the inscription Pilate had placed on the wooden sign nailed to the cross above Jesus' head. The gospel of John depicts the scene this way:

> Pilate also wrote an inscription and put it on the cross. It was written, "Jesus the Nazarene, The King of the Jews." Therefore many of the Jews read this inscription, for the place where Jesus was crucified was near the city; and it was written in Hebrew, Latin and in Greek. So the chief priests of the Jews were saying to Pilate, "Do not write, 'The King of the Jews'; but that He *said*, 'I am King of the Jews.'" Pilate answered, "What I have written I have written." (John 19:19–22, emphasis added)

Did Pilate have any idea that Christ was the Son of God? Possibly. Matthew suggests that Pilate sensed the evil motives of the Jewish leaders:

> So when the people gathered together, Pilate said to them, "Whom do you want me to release for you? Barabbas, or Jesus who is called Christ?" *For he knew that because of envy they had handed Him over.* (27:17–18, emphasis added)

Also, Pilate's wife came to him during Jesus' trial and told him not to have anything to do with sentencing Jesus to death. Here are her words, as recorded in Matthew 27:19:

While he was sitting on the judgment seat, his wife sent him a message, saying, "Have nothing to do with that righteous Man; for last night I suffered greatly in a dream because of Him."

Pilate sensed the gravity of the situation and symbolically washed his hands of the whole affair in Matthew 27:24. Deep down inside, he may have wondered if Jesus truly was the Messiah that the Jews had been waiting for. So he allowed the sign to stand: "This is Jesus the King of the Jews" (Matt. 27:37). And this statement alone may have brought one of the thieves to faith in Christ.

Jesus' Silence in the Face of His Accusers

Another explanation is that the meekness and humility Jesus maintained throughout the grueling ordeal may have stirred him to believe. Jesus did not defend Himself, even in the face of those who interrogated, slandered, attacked, and physically abused Him. His astonishing silence was prophesied hundreds of years earlier by the prophet Isaiah:

> He was oppressed and He was afflicted,
> Yet He did not open His mouth;
> Like a lamb that is led to slaughter,
> And like a sheep that is silent before its shearers,
> So He did not open His mouth. (Isa. 53:7)

Jesus' willingness to respond with love to the people who were carrying out His execution was an incredible testimony that He truly *was* the Son of God. Perhaps this gentle response moved the heart of one hardened criminal to believe.

Knowledge of Prophecies Concerning the Messiah

The men who were crucified with Jesus were undoubtedly familiar with the Scriptures that prophesied the coming of the Messiah. Whether they were Jewish or not, they knew that the Jews had long anticipated the coming of their King.

Perhaps the unfolding of the events leading up to Jesus' crucifixion triggered a memory of Scriptures that one of these men had heard before. Maybe he had read the story himself as a child and realized suddenly that everything was happening just as the Scriptures foretold regarding the birth, ministry, and death of the promised Messiah.

Whatever the case, God had uniquely prepared one of these men for this fateful moment, and the repentant thief expressed a genuine belief in the Savior. Darrell Bock notes:

> It is often said that the thief on the cross does not evidence his faith, for he has the equivalent of a deathbed conversion. But the testimony he gives for Jesus in his last moments is one of the most eloquent evidences of faith in the Bible.
> . . . The criminal anticipates the restoration and resurrection. He asks to be included. His depth of perception stands in contrast to the blindness of those who taunt. This man, despite a life full of sin, comes to Jesus and seeks forgiveness in his last mortal moments. He confesses his guilt and casts himself on Jesus' mercy and saving power. Luke could not have painted a clearer portrait of God's grace.[3]

Let's examine three critical aspects of this repentant criminal's confession.

First, *He knew he was a guilty sinner.* "And we indeed are suffering justly, for we are receiving what we deserve for our deeds" (Luke 23:41a). Acknowledging his sinful condition moved him to a crisis of belief.

Second, *He recognized the uniqueness of Jesus.* "But this man has done nothing wrong" (v. 41b). The criminal recognized that Jesus was no ordinary human being—He was the blameless Son of God.

Third, *He realized his eternal destiny was enjoined to Christ.* "Jesus, remember me when You come in Your kingdom" (v. 42). With these faith-filled words, he crowned Jesus as King of his own life and Master over his eternal destiny. This stirring, simple confession of faith brought a dying sinner out of sin's darkness into the glorious dawn of eternal life.

The Promise of Heaven

> "Truly I say to you, today you shall be with Me in Paradise." (Luke 23:43b)

In response to his faith, Jesus offered the repentant criminal

---

3. Darrell L. Bock, *Luke*, The IVP New Testament Commentary Series, ed. Grant R. Osborne (Downers Grove, Ill.: InterVarsity Press, 1994), p. 375.

eternal life. In the final horrifying moments of these men's lives, one believed and found life in Jesus' name. Again Darrell Bock observes:

> Jesus' reply gives the man more than he bargained for in terms of acceptance. The thief hopes that one day in the future he will share in Jesus' rule. Instead, Jesus promises him paradise from the moment of his death: *"I tell you the truth, today you will be with me in paradise."* The "truly I say to you" formula represents Jesus' most solemn way to reassure his neighbor. Faith's confession and request have been heard. . . . Jesus does not explain how this will work, but the assurance he gives to the thief is clear. Ironically, though dying amidst mocking, Jesus has saved while on the cross.[4]

Four Practical Truths

Among the rich theological truths embedded in this story are four practical principles for our Christian lives, especially in our relationships with unbelievers.

First, *no one is ever too far gone to become a Christian*. Regardless of his or her sin, no individual is beyond the reach of God's grace. The story of the thief on the cross settles that once and for all. As Barclay says, "it is literally true that while there is life there is hope."[5]

Second, *the printed page and the godly life are the two most effective tools for evangelism.* The New Testament teaches that the Word of God is powerful and able to affect change in the human heart (Heb. 4:12). But no less powerful than the witness of the Scriptures is the testimony of a holy life (Matt. 5:16; Eph. 5:8–9).

Third, *all that God wants and accepts is simple faith.* We bring nothing to God except our faith in Him and in the finished work of Christ on the cross. The criminal hanging alongside Jesus was not ushered into paradise on the basis of anything he had done. It was God's grace that opened the door for him, and His grace opens the door for us as well (Eph. 2:8–9; Rom. 10:8–9).

---

4. Bock, *Luke,* pp. 375–376.

5. Barclay, *The Gospel of Luke,* p. 287.

Fourth, *never doubt your instant acceptance into God's family when you open your heart to Him.* No amount of sin and wickedness can trump the grace of God. Satan loves to distract us by reminding us of our past failures. But in Christ we have power to overcome Satan and to master the guilt of our sin (see Rev. 12:10–11). James promises that if we resist Satan's advances, he will flee from us (James 4:7).

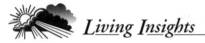 *Living Insights*

Luke's gospel rings with one grand theme from beginning to end: Salvation comes to all through faith in Jesus. In fact, as one writer frames it, salvation is the theme of the dying Savior's work:

> The question that arises from what Luke has shown us so far is a portentous one. He has emphasized, not by crude underlinings at the crucifixion itself but by the whole tenor of his story, that its great aim is accomplished when Jesus dies on the cross. But he has also made it quite clear that that death was not the penalty of the sins of Jesus; for he had none. And the question is this: If it was not his own sins which nailed him to the cross, *then what did?*[6]

Anyone who encounters the Gospel of Jesus Christ must wrestle with this probing question. The answer, of course, is that Christ died to pay the penalty for the sins of the whole world. This is the crux of the Gospel—and we must either believe or reject it. There are no other options to consider.

But this powerful story of suffering, faith, and salvation does raise some interesting questions. If one thief got the message, why did the other die in unbelief? Didn't he hear the same things the other heard? Had he not heard Jesus pray for His tormentors just as the other had heard? And how could an angry crowd of seemingly religious people completely reject what a godless criminal ultimately embraced?

These questions warrant some thoughtful reflection, so let's take time to examine more closely some of the theological themes Luke has laid out for us in this story.

6. Michael Wilcock, *The Message of Luke: The Saviour of the World,* The Bible Speaks Today Series (Downers Grove, Ill.: InterVarsity Press, 1979), p. 202.

Does our salvation only benefit us in the afterlife? Or is there a dimension of eternal life Christians experience before death? Read John 17:1–3; Ephesians 1:3–6; and Colossians 2:9–14. What conclusion can you draw from these passages?

_____

_____

_____

_____

_____

_____

What is at the root of spiritual blindness? What is the cause of unbelief? How do you explain the vicious acts of religious people and their unwillingness to believe in Messiah? See John 3:19; Romans 1:18–23; 2:5; 8; and 2 Corinthians 4:4.

_____

_____

_____

_____

_____

On a more practical note, how could you use what you've learned from our study of Luke 23:33–43 to share the Gospel with an unbeliever? What would you tell that person if they asked you what is required for them to have eternal life? In what ways could your own life be a more vibrant witness for Christ?

_____

_____

_____

_____

Questions for Group Reflection

1. If you had been present at the time of Jesus' death, what do you think you would have done? What would your response have been to the events of His crucifixion and death, and why?

2. What have you learned through this study about the ministry and the suffering of Jesus that you did not know before? How has it changed you?

3. What truths can you glean about salvation from this study? What are the requirements for salvation and eternal life, according to the Bible?

4. What can you discern about the character of God from Jesus' interaction with the two thieves on the cross?

5. Spend some time in prayer together, thanking God for who He is and for willingly offering up His Son, Jesus, as a sacrifice for your sin.

Chapter 10

"BEHOLD, YOUR SON!
BEHOLD, YOUR MOTHER!"

John 19:23–27

Imagine yourself transported through time to Calvary. If you had been present on that sunless afternoon when Christ died, would you be numbered among the gawking crowd, eager for a macabre thrill? Would you be found hiding in the shadows, only half-convinced of His innocence, yet sympathizing with His horrible suffering? Would you be in the midst of the huddle of Roman soldiers, engaged in a rousing game of chance? Or would you round out the band of curious tourists in Jerusalem for Passover, taking in a Roman crucifixion?

Maybe you'd be with Jesus' mother and His aunt, along with Mary Magdalene and the apostle John, standing faithfully near the cross so Jesus wouldn't die alone.

Surely, John, the gospel writer, hoped we'd all wrestle with the question of where we would have been on that fateful day. For in this poignant story, we gain a deeper awareness of the Savior's incredible sacrifice for our sins. And we also discover a clearer picture of ourselves.

The Connection

> Then the soldiers, when they had crucified Jesus, took His outer garments and made four parts, a part to every soldier and also the tunic; now the tunic was seamless, woven in one piece. So they said to one another, "Let us not tear it, but cast lots for it, to decide whose it shall be"; this was to fulfill the Scripture:, "They divided My outer garments among them, and for My clothing they cast lots." Therefore the soldiers did these things. (John 19:23–25a)

According to custom, the clothes of an executed criminal were at the disposal of his executioners. D. A. Carson provides some helpful perspective on this detail:

> Normally a Jew in Palestine wore a tunic (*chiton*)

85

next to the skin, and an outer garment, something like a robe (*to himation*, always in the singular). Here John tells us that they divided Jesus' *clothes* (*himatia*, that is the plural form) into four parts. If, somewhat anomalously, we are to think this plural form refers to the outer garment, then presumably the soldiers divided it into four parts, probably at the seams. But is more likely that the plural expression refers to Jesus' clothes, including a belt, sandals and head covering. . . . That left the tunic (*chiton*, NIV 'undergarment', but it was not equivalent to our undergarments, even though it was worn next to the skin, but to our suit, over which an outer garment might be worn), and it was decided to gamble for that item so it would not have to be dismembered—a sad loss since this garment *was seamless, woven in one piece from top to bottom*.[1]

The New Testament book of Hebrews describes Jesus as our "High Priest" (Heb. 4:14). John may have intended us to notice a link between the garment the high priest would have worn—the tunic, also woven in one piece from top to bottom—and the garment worn by Christ. Up to the time of Jesus' death, the priest presented sacrifices to the Lord on behalf of the sins of His people. But no priest had ever *become* the sacrifice. Until this One.

John's description of Jesus' tunic may have been intended as a bridge into his discussion of Jesus' words to His mother and the "beloved disciple," who was John himself. Jewish mothers customarily made *chitons*, or tunics, for their sons to commemorate their coming of age. It's likely Mary, Jesus' mother, did just that. It would have been a special gift of endearment from a mother to her son. And when the soldiers began talking about how they'd settle the matter of the tunic, Jesus naturally turned to see His mother's reaction. Notice the flow of the narrative:

> So they said to one another, "Let us not tear it, but cast lots for it, to decide whose it shall be"; this was to fulfill the Scripture:, "They divided My outer garments among them, and for My clothing they cast

1. D. A. Carson, *The Gospel According to John* (Grand Rapids, Mich.: William B. Eerdmans Publishing Company, 1991), p. 612.

lots. Therefore the soldiers did these things.

But standing by the cross of Jesus were His mother, and His mother's sister, Mary the wife of Clopas, and Mary Magdalene. When Jesus then saw His mother . . . (John 19:24–26a)

Here lies a striking contrast. Jesus, the innocent Lamb of God, dying a horrible death for the sins of the world, saw below Him callous Roman soldiers gambling for His clothes! A seamless garment meant more to these godless men than the Savior of the world. But John tells us that Jesus fixed His agonizing gaze on His mother, who was standing nearby.

What a remarkable tribute to His mother's love for Him and her faith in His work! For a Jewish Christian, standing by the cross of Jesus and aligning oneself with Him was perilous, yet Mary stood in quiet allegiance to her son and Savior. It must have been a remarkable scene to behold, and it was one that the Spirit of God compelled John to record. A. W. Pink captures it best:

> Here we see displayed the Mother-heart. She is the Dying Man's mother. The One who agonizes there on the Cross is her Child. She it was who first planted kisses on that brow now crowned with thorns. She it was who guided those hands and feet in their first infantile movements. No mother ever suffered as she did. His disciples may desert Him, and His friends may forsake Him, His nation may despise Him, but His mother stands there at the foot of His Cross. Oh, who can fathom or analyze the Mother-heart.[2]

Surely, John meant for us to see this portrait of Mary as Jesus' brokenhearted, yet loyal mother. But more importantly, he wanted us to consider Jesus' dying words to His mother and friend.

The Charge

> When Jesus then saw His mother, and the disciple whom He loved standing nearby, He said to His mother, "Woman, behold, your son!" Then He said

2. Arthur W. Pink, *The Seven Sayings of the Saviour on the Cross* (1958; reprint, Grand Rapids, Mich.: Baker Book House, 1976), pp. 49–50.

to the disciple, "Behold, your mother!" (John 19:26–27a)

Jesus, the dying Savior of the world, suffering unimaginable physical and mental agony, remained mindful of His mother. Why would He command that they take on these new roles? Most likely, Jesus' earthly father, Joseph, died when Jesus was a boy. Otherwise, he would have been the natural caregiver for Mary. Jesus' brothers— James, Joseph, Simon and Judas—had apparently rejected Him, and were perhaps unwilling to care for their mother:

> Now the feast of the Jews, the Feast of Booths, was near. Therefore His brothers said to Him, "Leave here and go into Judea, so that Your disciples also may see Your works which You are doing. For no one does anything in secret when he himself seeks to be known publicly. If You do these things, show Yourself to the world." For not even His brothers were believing in Him. (John 7:2–5. Compare Matt. 13:54–58 and Mark 3:21)

With His father dead and His siblings unbelievers, Jesus turned to His closest follower, John. In essence, Jesus inaugurated a new relationship between His mother, Mary, and his beloved friend. Mary would be John's mother; John would be her son.

The Response

> From that hour the disciple took her into his own household. (John 19:27b)

Though wonderfully courageous in her faith, Mary needed the support and care of a loving family. Jesus made provision for that moments before His death. And John, "the disciple whom Jesus loved," immediately responded to Jesus' charge by taking Mary to his own household. Literally, the Greek text says, "the disciple took her into his own," meaning his own family and his own world. Mary became intimately a part of John's family from that moment on.

Three Principles of Application

This passage contains several great spiritual and theological truths. Let's take a closer look at three principles from this story that we can apply to our personal lives.

First, *grace extends to those who have failed.* John is listed among the disciples who actually fled for safety when they realized that Jesus was being taken into custody (see Mark 14:50). Though he described himself as Jesus' beloved disciple, John, too, allowed fear to shrink his faith.

Yet, he returned to stand near Jesus as He died at Calvary. The last words John heard from Jesus' lips weren't words of condemnation for his fickle faith. Instead, He heard a loving admonition to initiate a new relationship with Mary, the mother of Jesus. What confidence Jesus extended to John in that mournful hour of agony and suffering! Clearly, though John ranked among the deserters, Jesus trusted him with the care of His mother.

Second, *spiritual bonds are stronger than natural bonds.* You may recall Jesus' puzzling statement at the end of His parables of the sower and of the lamp in Luke 8:21. He said, "My mother and My brothers are these who hear the word of God and do it." Jesus knew that those individuals related to Him by faith comprised His true family, and were often closer than even His birth relatives.

Practically speaking, pastors, teachers, youth leaders, and believers in general often feel closer to their fellow brothers and sisters in Christ than to their blood relatives. Jesus enjoyed an intimate, abiding relationship with John that surpassed His ties to His siblings who had rejected Him. So it was natural that Jesus turned to His spiritual family in His darkest hour.

Third, *the principle of perpetual parental respect is to be obeyed.* The New Testament clearly teaches believers to establish and maintain lifelong respect for their parents. This may, in some instances, require caring for them in their advanced age (see Prov. 23:22). Even as the life drained from His body, Jesus honored His mother and considered her welfare above His own.

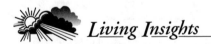 *Living Insights*

King Solomon wrote:

> Listen to your father who begot you,
> And do not despise your mother when she is old.
> (Prov. 23:22)

For those of us who have traded harsh memories of a painful childhood for years of bitterness and anger toward one or both parents, these are penetrating words. Problems in our families can leave us wounded, disillusioned, disappointed, and fearful of reaching out to others because of fear of rejection.

Sadly, in our culture, loneliness ranks among the most common sources of depression and death among the elderly. Countless nursing homes and retirement centers around the country provide shelter and care for some of the most lonely and forsaken people on the planet. Most of these people have children or other family members still living. However, their relatives are often too distracted, busy, or bitter to take the time to visit or call.

Yet the Bible clearly teaches that God honors those who care for their own, especially children who provide for their parents. Exodus 20:12 contains this command:

> "Honor your father and your mother, that your days
> may be prolonged in the land which the Lord your
> God gives you."

This is the first of the Ten Commandments to contain a promise: God will bless you when you honor your parents! Take some time now to reflect on your relationship with your earthly parents. Ask yourself the following questions:

What was my relationship with my parents like when I was growing up? What was positive about it? What was difficult about it?

_____

_____

_____

_____

_____

_____

In what ways does my current relationship with my mother, father, brothers, and sisters honor the Lord? In what ways do my actions and attitudes *not* honor the Lord? Have I experienced any situations which have caused me to harbor resentment toward my parents or other family members?

_____

_____

_____

_____

_____

_____

Have I experienced hurts for which I may need to grant for-giveness? Are there situations for which I need to *seek* forgiveness from a parent or family member? What practical steps can I take to restore these relationships?

_____

_____

_____

_____

_____

How can I clearly demonstrate my love for my friends and family?

_____

_____

_____

_____

What is my attitude toward members of my spouse's family? What can I do to improve my relationship with them and to show honor to them?

_____

_____

_____

_____

Prayerfully ask the Lord to search your heart for areas that need adjustment. Lift those attitudes up to Him, and ask for forgiveness if that is your need. Take the steps necessary to seek restoration of your vital relationships. Remember—it's never too late to start doing what's right!

 ## Questions for Group Reflection

1. Describe the environment in your home growing up. Did you grow up in a Christian family? What was your relationship like with your parents? With your brothers and sisters? With your extended family?

2. What was one difficult experience you had growing up? How did you deal with it? What was the response of your family and friends to the situation? To whom did you turn when you needed help? What was the outcome?

3. How would you describe Jesus' relationship with his mother? His brothers? His friend John? What have you learned about relationships from Jesus' interaction with His relatives and friends in this passage?

4. Take some time now to pray for God's help in restoring any broken relationships.

Chapter 11

"WHY HAVE YOU FORSAKEN ME?"

Matthew 27:45–46

Nature did its duty that afternoon, providing a fitting backdrop for the grim scene. A cloudless, sunlit sky would have been incongruous with the unfolding drama. So God chose a dark background to emphasize the darkness of the moment.

The great mystery lies in the depth of anguish that Jesus expressed in His death cry: "My God, My God, why have You forsaken Me?" The darkness Jesus felt was real and palpable as God the Father turned His back on His Son, who bore the sins of the world. For a period of time, the great Light of the World flickered . . . and eventually went out.

As we wrestle with this difficult passage, we will gain a sense of the pain Jesus endured because of our sin. And we will also discover why the Father, in His mysterious and eternal plan, allowed such great darkness to briefly overshadow His Son's marvelous light.

The Setting

> Now from the sixth hour darkness fell upon all
> the land until the ninth hour. (Matt. 27:45)

From noon until the time of Christ's death at around 3:00 P.M., a blanket of heavy darkness hung like a canopy over Israel. It literally "fell upon all the land" as evidence of God's judgment for sin taken on by His Son, Jesus, on the cross.[1]

Some scholars try to explain away this darkness by suggesting that it was caused by an eclipse or other natural occurrence. But this was no mere eclipse! Clearly, this was a startling supernatural phenomenon which, coupled with a violent earthquake, caused even the hardened Roman soldiers at the foot of the cross to acknowledge fearfully, "Truly this *was* the Son of God!" (Matt. 27:54, emphasis added)

---

1. Leon Morris, *The Gospel according to Matthew* (Grand Rapids, Mich.: William B. Eerdmans Publishing Company, 1992), p. 720.

The Desperate Cry

> About the ninth hour Jesus cried out with a loud voice, saying, *"Eli, Eli, lama sabachthani?"* that is, "My God, My God, why have You forsaken Me?" (v.46)

In the darkness, Jesus let out a haunting cry—a question which portrayed His profound sense of abandonment in His loneliest hour. Author Raymond Brown points out:

> . . . Jesus has been abandoned by his disciples and mocked by all who have come to the cross. Darkness has covered the earth; there is nothing that shows God acting on Jesus' side. How appropriate that Jesus feel forsaken! His "Why?" is that of someone who has plumbed the depths of the abyss, and feels enveloped by the power of darkness. Jesus is not questioning the existence of God or the power of God to do something about what is happening; he is questioning the silence of the one whom he calls "My God."[2]

But God had been silent before. Clearly, something more was at stake here. To better understand what motivated His heart-wrenching question, let's take a closer look at Jesus' words.

They Were Screamed Out

Apparently, those around Jesus heard His agonizing cry from the cross. Some misunderstood it as an appeal to the prophet Elijah for help, but what Jesus actually said came from Psalm 22:

> My God, my God, why have You forsaken me?
> Far from my deliverance are the words of my
>   groaning.
> O my God, I cry by day, but You do not answer;
> And by night, but I have no rest. (Ps. 22:1–2)

Jesus' death cry carried a tone of desperation. In fact, the word Matthew uses is *anaboan*, which means "to cry out or scream in a loud voice." One commentator notes:

> The range of *boan* and *anaboan* includes solemn

---

2. Raymond E. Brown, *The Death of the Messiah: From Gethsemane to the Grave* (New York, N.Y.: Doubleday, 1994), vol. 2, p. 1046.

proclamation, the acclamation or shout of a crowd, and a desperate cry for help. . . . Clearly, then, the scream and loud cry lend desperate urgency to Jesus' petition. Moreover, to those familiar with crucifixion, such a cry would not have seemed unusual. Blinzler (*Trial* 261) describes as part of what made crucifixions particularly gruesome "the screams of rage and pain, the wild curses and outbreaks of nameless despair of the unhappy victims." Yet it was not in rage but in prayer that Jesus screamed his loud cry, even as the martyrs in Rev. 6:10 shouted with a loud cry their prayer for God to intervene.[3]

They Were Recorded Exactly as He Said Them

Jesus spoke His death cry in Aramaic, the language of His youth. This may be why some of the Romans misunderstood Him. Jesus had undoubtedly learned the Psalms by heart as a young Jewish lad, and He remembered Psalm 22 in Aramaic. As one scholar notes:

> The words *Eli, Eli,* which Matthew translates "my God, my God," are a Greek transliteration of the Hebrew (Mark has *Eloi, Eloi,* which is Aramaic, as are the words *lema sabachthani*). When the non-Jewish soldiers under the cross heard the cry, they said, "This man calls Elijah." The difference between *"Eli"* and "Elijah" has caused people to ask why the soldiers thought Jesus was calling the Old Testament prophet. A study of the Dead Sea Scroll of Isaiah has shown that the old Hebrew possessive suffix *−iya* was still in use in the time of Christ. Jesus most likely said, *"Eliya, Eliya"* ("my God, my God").[4]

In His darkest hour, Jesus turned to David's impassioned plea in Psalm 22 and made it His own. These mysterious words have become "a saying before which we must bow in reverence, and yet at the same time we must try to understand."[5]

---

3. Brown, *The Death of the Messiah*, p. 1044.

4. Erich H. Kiehl, *The Passion of Our Lord* (Grand Rapids, Mich.: Baker Book House Company, 1990), p. 137.

5. William Barclay, *The Gospel of Matthew*, rev. ed., The Daily Study Bible Series (Philadelphia, Pa.: The Westminster Press, 1975), vol. 2, p. 368.

They Reveal Estrangement between Jesus and His Father

For the first time, Jesus did not appeal to the Lord as "Father." Instead, He called Him "my God." The first evidence emerges here that a breach has occurred between Jesus and the Father, who have existed inextricably as one throughout eternity. For the first time in His life on earth, Jesus experienced separation from His Father in heaven. But why would the Father forsake His Son at the time when He needed strength and support the most? Two important passages, one in the Old Testament and one in the New Testament, provide us with the answer.

Psalm 22 proclaims God's absolute holiness and majesty:

> Yet You are holy,
> O You who are enthroned upon the praises of Israel.
> (Ps. 22:3)

Since God is holy, He cannot look upon sin. So when Christ took upon Himself the sins of the world on the cross, God "turned His back" on His Son. But how could this be? How could God the Father, even in all His holiness, turn away from His beloved Son? The apostle Paul explained the glorious mystery of substitutionary atonement for our sin this way:

> He made Him who knew no sin to be sin on our behalf, so that we might become the righteousness of God in Him. (2 Cor. 5:21)

Sin alienated humanity from the holiness of the Father. At the point at which Jesus became the offering for the sins of the world, He was separated from God. Jesus' anguished words gave a penetrating voice to that grim reality. God simply could not fellowship with sin. D. A. Carson notes:

> If we ask in what ontological [metaphysical] sense the Father and the Son are here divided, the answer must be that we do not know because we are not told. If we ask for what purpose they are divided, the ultimate answer must be tied in with Gethsemane, the Last Supper, passion passages such as [Matthew] 1:21; 20:28 (see also 26:26–29, 39–44), and the theological interpretation articulated by Paul (for example, Rom. 3:21–26). In this cry of dereliction, the horror of the world's sin and the

cost of our salvation are revealed. In the words of Elizabeth Browning:

> Yea, once Immanuel's orphaned cry his universe
> hath shaken.
> It went up single, echoless, "My God, I am
> forsaken!"
> It went up from the Holy's lips amid his lost
> creation,
> That, of the lost, no son should use those words
> of desolation.[6]

In His death, Christ experienced the ultimate penalty for sin, separation from God, which for Him was the greatest agony of all. As believers, we will *never* know such suffering. And we have the assurance that even when we are tested, God will never turn His back on us. Christ endured that agonizing separation so that we would never have to.

The Sacrifice of Christ

The prevailing image in the New Testament book of Hebrews is that of sacrifices being offered to atone for sin. Writing to Jewish believers, the writer understood that Christ's ministry as High Priest would resonate deeply with those who had formerly worshiped at the temple (see Ps. 110:4, Heb. 3:1, 5:1–6, 10). Suffering under the threat of persecution, these converts were tempted to return to their old ways of worshiping, rather than face serious consequences. They needed a good reason not to go back. So this wise pastor wrote boldly that Christ had provided the better way:

> Then He said, "Behold, I have come to do Your will."
> He takes away the first in order to establish the
> second. By this will we have been sanctified through
> the offering of the body of Jesus Christ *once for all.*
> Every priest stands daily ministering and offering
> time after time the same sacrifices, which can never
> take away sins; *but He, having offered one sacrifice for
> sins for all time, sat down at the right hand of God.*
> (Heb. 10:9–12, emphasis added)

---

6. D. A. Carson, "Matthew," in *The Expositor's Bible Commentary*, ed. Frank E. Gaebelein (Grand Rapids, Mich.: Zondervan Publishing House, 1984), p. 579.

The work of sacrifice has been done—*once for all*. This is the essence of the Gospel! The work was finished for us by Jesus Christ on the cross. We need not fear the penalty of sin. And there is an added benefit, according to Hebrews 13:

> . . . for He Himself has said, "*I will never desert you, nor will I ever forsake you.*" (v. 5b, emphasis added)

As believers, we will never know the feeling of utter abandonment. We will never be forsaken as Christ was forsaken. He bore our reproach on the cross that day. What tender, comforting words these are to us who have believed!

> The soul that on Jesus hath leaned for repose
> I will not, I will not desert to his foes;
> That soul, tho' all hell should endeavor to shake,
> I'll never, no never, no never forsake.[7]

A desperate cry from the Savior's lips was transformed for us into an eternal song of hope and joyful confidence. God will never leave us or forsake us!

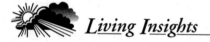 *Living Insights*

A fitting close to our time on Golgotha's lonely hill is provided by writer Ken Gire. Take a moment to ponder these words, taken from his meditation on Jesus' anguished cry and Psalm 22:

> Beautiful Savior,
>
> Thank you for the prophetic picture of your sufferings that was foreshadowed through the life of your servant David. Certainly those words were on your heart as you hung on that God-forsaken cross. Give me a few undistracted minutes with that picture, Lord, so I may stand silently before you now the way that centurion did so many years ago. And slowly, a line at a time, let my eyes, as his eyes did, read the battered prose of this most sacred prayer.

---

7. "How Firm a Foundation," from John Rippon's *Selection of Hymns*, 1787, in *Sing to the Lord* (Kansas City, Mo.: Lillenas Publishing Company, 1993), no. 689

My God, my God, why have you forsaken me?
    Why are you so far from . . . me,
        so far from the words of my groaning?
O my God, I cry out by day, but you do not
    answer,
        by night, and am not silent.
Yet you are enthroned as the Holy One;
    you are the praise of Israel.
In you our fathers put their trust;
    they trusted and you delivered them.
They cried to you and were saved;
    in you they trusted and were not disappointed.

But I am a worm and not a man,
    scorned by men and despised by the people.
All who see me mock me;
    they hurl insults, shaking their heads:
"He trusts in the Lord;
    let the Lord rescue him.
Let him deliver him,
    since he delights in him."

Yet you brought me out of the womb;
    you made me trust in you
        even at my mother's breast.
From birth I was cast upon you;
    from my mother's womb you have been
    my God.
Do not be far from me,
    for trouble is near
        and there is no one to help.

Many bulls surround me;
    strong bulls of Bashan encircle me.
Roaring lions tearing their prey
    open their mouths wide against me.
I am poured out like water,
    and all my bones are out of joint.
My heart has turned to wax;
    it has melted away within me.
My strength is dried up like a postherd,
    and my tongue sticks to the roof of my mouth;

you lay me in the dust of death.
Dogs have surrounded me;
    a band of evil men has encircled me,
    they have pierced my hands and my feet.
I can count all my bones;
    people stare and gloat over me.
They divide my garments among them
    and cast lots for my clothing.

But you, O Lord, be not far off;
    O my Strength, come quickly to help me.
Deliver my life from the sword,
    my precious life from the power of the dogs.
Rescue me from the mouth of the lions;
    save me from the horns of the wild oxen.

I will declare your name to my brothers;
    in the congregation I will praise you.
You who fear the Lord, praise him!
All you descendants of Jacob, honor him!
Revere him, all you descendants of Israel!
For he has not despised or disdained
    the suffering of the afflicted one;
    he has not hidden his face from him
    but has listened to his cry for help.[8]

Before you close this chapter, bow before the Lord in prayer. Thank Him for His grace and mercy offered to you through Christ's sacrificial death at Calvary. Then renew your commitment to walk in a manner worthy of the tremendous price He paid for you.

 Questions for Group Reflection

1. What about Jesus' cry of "Why have You forsaken me?" impacts you the most? Why?

2. Have you ever felt like God had turned His back on you? What were the circumstances? What made you realize that He still

8. Ken Gire, *Intense Moments with the Savior: Learning to Feel* (Grand Rapids, Mich.: Zondervan Publishing House, 1994), pp. 124–126.

loved you? How did you know that He was still there?

3. What have you learned about the character of Jesus from this chapter? The character of God the Father? Have any of your previous views of God been challenged?

4. What have you discovered about God's holiness from His interaction with Jesus on the cross? How has your understanding of Jesus' suffering deepened?

Spend some time now thanking God for His mercy and love. Reflect prayerfully on the incredible sacrifice that Jesus Christ made on the cross, and praise Him for offering His life for you.

Chapter 12

"I AM THIRSTY"

John 19:28–29

Jesus' earthbound journey ended in unimaginable suffering. For the most part, our Lord journeyed alone through His long days of temptation in the wilderness, His solitary hours spent in anguished prayer among the olive trees, and His last horrifying moments on the cross.

Jesus' humanity is emphasized by the seven sayings that He uttered from the cross before His death; they illustrate clearly that Christ was one of us. There can be no doubt that He was not only God, but also very much a man.

Jesus' fifth saying from the cross, "I am thirsty," reveals His intense physical suffering. This anguished cry rang out as Christ hung suspended between heaven and earth. In it, He expresses one of humanity's most primal needs—the need to have our thirst quenched.

Jesus is often referred to by scholars as *theanthropic*. This term is a combination of two Greek words, *theos* for "God" and *anthropos* for "man." In his letter to the church in Philippi, Paul fleshed out the meaning of this theological concept:

> Have this attitude in yourselves which was also in Christ Jesus, who, although He existed in the form of God, did not regard equality with God a thing to be grasped, but emptied Himself, taking the form of a bond-servant, and being made in the likeness of men. Being found in appearance as a man, He humbled Himself by becoming obedient to the point of death, even death on a cross. (Phil. 2:5–8)

Christ "emptied Himself" of His glory to come to earth. He took all His rights as God and "poured them out." He sacrificed His position at the right hand of the Father. He chose to leave the place where angels continually called out "Holy, Holy, Holy" around the throne, where even the seraphim covered their faces rather than dare to look at the living God.

This chapter has been adapted from "I Am Thirsty," in the Bible study guide *Christ's Agony and Ecstasy*, written by Ed Neuenschwander, from the Bible-teaching ministry of Charles R. Swindoll (Fullerton, Calif.: Insight for Living, 1982).

Though Jesus suffered greatly, in no way did His humanity diminish His deity. He was still fully God as well as fully man. As a man, He grew tired and fell asleep in the storm, but as deity He stilled the wind and calmed the sea. In His humanity, He wept at the tomb of Lazarus, yet as God, He called him back to life!

Let's look more closely at Jesus' fifth cry from the cross to gain a deeper understanding of what it really meant for the Word to become flesh and dwell among us (John 1:14).

A Grim Glimpse of Humanity

> After this, Jesus, knowing that all things had
> already been accomplished, to fulfill the Scripture,
> said, "I am thirsty." (John 19:28)

With stunning realism, John painted a vivid portrait of Christ's humanity: "He became thirsty." As part of His suffering on our behalf, Jesus endured the physiological processes set in motion by His crucifixion. Remarkably, even His thirst pointed to the fulfillment of prophecy concerning His death, and John noted that Jesus spoke "knowing that all things had already been accomplished."

The Greek word *oida* means "to know intuitively, innately; to have in mind the facts and then to recall them." Jesus possessed a perfect knowledge of the Scriptures. He understood all that had been predicted regarding His suffering and death, and He must have reviewed each of these prophecies in His final tortuous hours on the cross. As He did, He checked off each one in His mind and marked them "fulfilled." One that surely came to mind was Psalm 69:

> Reproach has broken my heart and I am so sick.
> And I looked for sympathy, but there was none,
> And for comforters, but I found none.
> They also gave me gall for my food
> And for my thirst they gave me vinegar to drink.
> (Psalm 69:20–21)

David's words of desperation in this psalm foreshadowed the Messiah's death that would occur centuries later. As Roman soldiers lifted wine to Jesus' parched and bleeding lips, once again the Scriptures were fulfilled (v. 29).

This was not the first time that Jesus had experienced intense thirst and was offered relief. Matthew 27:34 and Mark 15:23 point to an earlier time when the soldiers had offered Him wine to quench

His burning thirst. However, this had been a *fresh* wine mixed with gall. This mixture acted as a narcotic, designed to ease the horrific pain. Fresh wine made the otherwise bitter potion somewhat palatable, so the victim wouldn't gag. Still, Jesus had refused to drink it.

Just prior to Christ's death, soldiers offered Him wine again. However, this was *sour* wine that had been left standing in a jar at the site. No doubt the basin had been placed there as a cheap source of refreshment for the soldiers on duty and to provide some measure of relief to the condemned.

Having sipped the bitter drink, Jesus uttered two final statements, hung His battered head, and died. His ordeal ended, as the Savior of the world died an all-too-human death.

Three Observations

Three practical observations worth noting emerge from this passage.

First, *Christ's true humanity was displayed*. The One who had promised living water to the woman at the well died thirsty. This is the amazing paradox of the Incarnation—God accomplished redemption by becoming like the ones needing to be redeemed. Perhaps this thought inspired the author of the book of Hebrews to write:

> For we do not have a high priest who cannot sympathize with our weaknesses, but One who has been tempted in all things as we are, yet without sin. (Hebrews 4:15)

Only humans can be high priests. But only Christ could endure the agony and torture of the cross and emerge blameless. Because Jesus suffered so much, He understands our humanity like no other. His words "I am thirsty" remind us that He understands the relentless burdens of what it means to be human.

Second, *Jesus began His ministry hungry and ended His ministry thirsty*. The Messiah's ministry was framed in humanity. In the wilderness, tempted by Satan, Jesus went without food for over a month. After emerging from His desert trial, His body no doubt showed signs of starvation and exposure to the harsh elements. But that in no way diminished His deity. Rather, it emphasized His humanity. He was "tempted in all things as we are, yet without sin."

The same is true of the gospel account of the end of Christ's ministry. He died bruised, bleeding, broken, and thirsty. His Messianic ministry culminated in abject human misery painfully unrelieved.

Finally, *the unselfishness of the Savior was plainly displayed.* Throughout the ordeal, Jesus thought of the needs of those around Him. In fact, up to this point, His words from the cross reflected His love for dying thieves and grieving loved ones rather than concern for Himself. At last, only moments before His death, Jesus asked for a drink, only to be offered cheap, discarded wine. He truly, completely, emptied Himself by becoming "obedient to the point of death, even death on a cross" (Phil. 2:8).

May we never recover from the wonder of Christ's cross and our unworthiness that made it necessary!

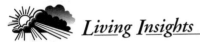 *Living Insights*

Author Judith Mattison offers some thought-provoking observations about the human aspect of Jesus' death:

> Jesus dragged his cross along the streets of Jerusalem toward the hill of his demise, for the most part, alone. There were none close by to encourage him, to cheer him on. Rather, people jeered him; insults and disgust fell on his bleeding brow. Simon of Cyrene was enlisted to help carry the heavy cross. It was the only comfort Jesus received. Then, as he hung on the cross, his simple request for water was met with an offering of vinegar. Cruelty. Why? Why was it that Jesus had no partner on this journey to death, no compassionate friend?
>
> . . . Why was he alone in his ultimate struggle? . . . What is it that God would have us know in this unfolding drama of abandonment, abuse, and pain?
>
> God would have us know that when Jesus asks for water, he is one of us. He is thirsty. He is human. He knows loneliness. He hurts, and he needs the power of God's love. Jesus is one of us.[1]

1. Judith Mattison, *The Seven Last Words of Christ: The Message of the Cross for Today* (Minneapolis, Minn.: Augsburg Press, 1992), p. 52.

And because He is one of us, He understands us intimately. Our fears. Our doubts. Our insecurities. Our disillusionment. Our pain. Nothing we feel slips past Jesus unnoticed. He knows us, and He loves us. And that's a hope-filled combination!

Ask yourself the following questions:

What hurts have I experienced in the past that may have made me feel sad, lonely, upset, angry, or misunderstood?

_____

_____

_____

_____

_____

How did I respond? To whom did I turn for counsel and advice? Did I seek God during that time? If so, how?

_____

_____

_____

What struggles are you experiencing in your life now? List any current circumstances that may be making you feel anxious. How can you apply to your own situation what you have learned about Jesus' suffering? What does God promise you in His Word?

_____

_____

_____

_____

Now get on your knees and lift up your burdens to your waiting Savior. He understands, and He loves you. Remember—He's one of us!

Questions for Group Reflection

1. Think of a time when you experienced a physical trial or suffering of some kind. What was the situation? How did you respond?

2. What do you feel was the most difficult part of Jesus' journey on earth? In what ways did He suffer as a man? If you had been in His place, what do you think would have been the hardest part for you?

3. Look up each of these verses: Isaiah 55:1; Psalm 22:14; 23:1; Jeremiah 2:13; Matthew 3:11; 10:42; 14:29; Luke 7:44; John 3:5; 4:10; Acts 1:5. How is water described in each verse? Is the term *water* used literally or figuratively? What does it symbolize? Explain.

4. Spend some time in prayer, thanking God for sending His Son to die for you. Offer thanksgiving to Jesus for His willingness to endure such severe physical suffering on your behalf.

Chapter 13
"IT IS FINISHED!"
John 19:30

Again, Jesus cried out with a loud voice. But this time, instead of a cry of desperate anguish, a cry of glorious victory sounded from His lips.

The scene may be better understood against the backdrop of two verses from Proverbs 13:

> Hope deferred makes the heart sick, but desire fulfilled is a tree of life. (v. 12)

> Desire realized is sweetness to the soul. (v. 19)

Jesus had reached His goal of atoning for human sin, all according to His Father's plan. The realization of God's desire was sweetness to Jesus' soul as He loudly and triumphantly proclaimed, "It is finished!"

It Is Finished

With conquering resolve, Jesus uttered the clarion cry of the ages, marking the end of sin's death-grip on the human soul. The work was done, the divine obligation to His Father's will fully satisfied. Throughout the gospel of John, the theme of fulfilled obligation emerges time and time again:

> Jesus said to them, "My food is to do the will of Him who sent Me and to *accomplish* His work." (John 4:34, emphasis added)

> "But the testimony which I have is greater than the testimony of John; for the works which the Father has given Me to *accomplish*—the very works that I do—testify about Me, that the Father has sent Me." (John 5:36, emphasis added)

> "I glorified You on the earth, having *accomplished* the work which You have given me to do." (John 17:4, emphasis added)

After this, Jesus, knowing that all things had already been *accomplished*, to fulfill Scripture, said, "I am thirsty." (John 19:28, emphasis added)

"It is *finished!*" (John 19:30, emphasis added)

Each of the verses above share a word set off in italics. The words translated *accomplished* and *finished* derive from the Greek term *teleo*, which means "to bring to an end, to complete, or to finish." According to author and pastor Warren Wiersbe, the expression *tetelestai*—"It is finished!"—was used commonly in Jesus' day:

> Though this word isn't recognized by most people in our contemporary world, it was a familiar word when our Lord was ministering on earth. Archaeologists have discovered many ancient Greek documents that help us better understand Bible words, because the New Testament was written in the common language of the Greek-speaking people of that day . . . If you were to consult the New Testament Greek lexicons, you would learn that common people in Jesus' day used the word "tetelestai" in their everyday lives.[1]

Wiersbe notes that this phrase was used by servants notifying their masters of a completed task and by priests as part of the temple worship, signifying a completed sacrifice. It was also used by artists who, having completed their work, "would step back, look at it, and say, 'Tetelestai—it is finished!'"[2]

Having fulfilled His divine task of redeeming the world, the King of Kings announced its completion with words even the lowliest servant could comprehend!

Understanding the Finished Work

To grasp the meaning of Christ's finished work, we must first understand His obligation to God. Hebrews 10:4–7 states it this way:

For it is impossible for the blood of bulls and goats

1. Warren W. Wiersbe, *The Cross of Jesus: What His Words from Calvary Mean for Us* (Grand Rapids, Mich.: Baker Books, 1997), p. 105.

2. Wiersbe, p. 107–108.

to take away sins. Therefore, when He comes into the world, He says, "Sacrifice and offering You have not desired, but a body You have prepared for Me; In whole burnt offerings and sacrifices for sin You have taken no pleasure.

Then I said, 'Behold, I have come (in the scroll of the book it is written of Me) to do Your will, O God.'"

Christ came to do His Father's will and to fulfill to the last detail all that God wanted Him to accomplish. Specifically, the Father's will was accomplished in four distinct areas.

Concerning the Atonement

Atonement is translated from the Hebrew word *kapar*, which means "to cover." God chose this way to deal with the sins of His people throughout the Old Testament period. Atonement occurred when the blood of bulls and goats was shed to "cover" (temporarily) the sins of the Israelites.

These animal sacrifices foreshadowed God's final and permanent dealing with human sin. The complete fulfillment of God's requirements for the remission of sins occurred when Jesus died in our place. He paid the price for our sins by becoming the ultimate sacrifice. The apostle Paul illustrates this great truth in his second letter to the Corinthians:

> He made Him who knew no sin to be sin on our behalf, so that we might become the righteousness of God in Him. (2 Cor. 5:21)

What assurance do we have that Jesus' death satisfied the Father's will? Our confidence comes from God's Word. The following four proofs provide clear evidence that His Son's death on the cross satisfied God's requirements for righteousness.

First, *the veil of the temple was torn in two from top to bottom*. Luke records this event in his gospel:

> It was now about the sixth hour, and darkness fell over the whole land until the ninth hour, because the sun was obscured; and the veil of the temple was torn in two. (23:44–45)

While the people lived under the weight of their sin, darkness reigned, separating humanity from a holy God. The immensely thick fabric of the temple veil forbade access to the Holy of Holies to everyone but the high priest, who entered once a year on the Day of Atonement to offer sacrifices for sin. The book of Hebrews describes how Christ, as our High Priest, provided us access to the Father:

> But when Christ appeared as a high priest of the good things to come, He entered through the greater and more perfect tabernacle, not made with hands, that is to say, not of this creation; and not through the blood of goats and calves, but through His own blood, He entered the holy place once for all, having obtained eternal redemption.
>
> For if the blood of goats and bulls and the ashes of a heifer sprinkling those who have been defiled sanctify for the cleansing of the flesh, how much more will the blood of Christ, who through the eternal Spirit offered Himself without blemish to God, cleanse your conscience from dead works to serve the living God? (Heb. 9:11–14)

What a marvelous thought! In His death, Christ tore through the heavy veil of death's darkness, giving us access to the shining light of God's presence. And He did it *once for all!*

Second, *Christ was raised from the dead.* The resurrection and the ascension demonstrated the sufficiency of Christ's death to save His people from their sins. His resurrection signified God's triumph over the grave.

Third, *Christ was accepted back into heaven.* After He rose from the dead, Jesus ascended to take His rightful place at the right hand of His Father. His triumphant return to glory reflected His decisive victory on the cross.

Fourth, *the Holy Spirit was sent after Christ ascended to the Father.* Having received His Son back into heaven, God sent the Holy Spirit as His divine exclamation point, fulfilling the promise Jesus made to His disciples to send a Helper in His place.

Concerning the Scriptures

Christ's death also completed God's will concerning the Scriptures:

> After this, Jesus, knowing that all things had

already been accomplished, to fulfill the Scripture, said, "I am thirsty." A jar full of sour wine was standing there; so they put a sponge full of the sour wine upon a branch of hyssop and brought it up to His mouth. Therefore when Jesus had received the sour wine, He said "It is finished!" And He bowed His head and gave up His spirit. (John 19:28–30)

Like one of Tchaikovsky's great masterpieces, Christ's death culminated in a symphony of prophetic movements in Scripture, all building toward a magnificent grand finale. Faithfully, obediently, without waver or complaint, Christ performed His Father's will.

Concerning the Law

Though the Law of Moses enriched the lives of devout Jewish people in many ways, it ultimately crushed them in its demands. Because no one could possibly keep all of God's commands perfectly, humanity slumped under the weight of condemnation.

But Christ's death changed everything. Paul makes this clear in the book of Romans:

For what the Law could not do, weak as it was through the flesh, God did: sending His own Son in the likeness of sinful flesh and as an offering for sin, He condemned sin in the flesh, so that the requirement of the Law might be fulfilled in us, who do not walk according to the flesh but according to the Spirit. (8:3–4)

And concerning the unbelieving Jewish people still trying to achieve righteousness under the law, Paul wrote:

For not knowing about God's righteousness [in Christ] and seeking to establish their own, they did not subject themselves to the righteousness of God. For Christ is the end of the law for righteousness to everyone who believes. (Rom. 10:3–4)

The Cross accomplished God's will by providing a new and better way to righteousness . . . a righteousness that comes through faith in Christ, setting sinners free from guilt's chains to walk in newness of life!

Concerning the Devil

> Therefore, since the children share in flesh and blood, He Himself likewise also partook of the same, that through death He might render powerless him who had the power of death, that is, the devil, and might free those who through fear of death were subject to slavery all their lives. (Heb. 2:14–15)

Christ's final cry of "It is finished!" confirmed God's eternal sentence on Satan, the enemy of our souls. Death and the grave, once powerful weapons in Satan's diabolic regime, were removed from his arsenal through Christ's overwhelming victory over sin. In one sweeping blow, God stripped Satan of his power and sealed his eternal fate.

A triumphant, finished work, indeed!

 *Living Insights*

Have you ever tried to play chess with a professional chess player? Every halting move on your part meets with a chuckle or insidious "Mmm-hmm" from your opponent. You realize there's no way out. With every move, you're just getting closer to the end.

Satan knows the feeling well. Every day, God says to him, "Mmm-hmm. You're one day closer to the end." The devil is defeated, and he knows it! But he wants to deceive you into thinking that what Christ did for you on the cross wasn't enough.

Ever feel like you're playing an impossible game of chess with your adversary, the devil? He fools you into thinking that you must make all the right moves by a being a better Christian, giving more, praying more, sinning less, witnessing more, and knowing your Bible better. "Make one false move and the game's over," he whispers, "You've lost God's favor."

Does Satan have you in a stranglehold of guilt? Is he constantly badgering you about a sinful habit from which you can't break free? Is he reminding you of a period in your life when you didn't honor the Lord by the way you lived? He loves to use the mistakes of your past to hound you until you break. It's one of his favorite strategies. Just remember: you can't disarm Satan in the strength of the flesh, but you can resist his advances through Christ in the power of the Cross!

Thoughtfully consider the following questions:

Are there areas in your life in which you experience repeated failure? Does guilt from your past dog your every attempt to gain ground in your relationship with Christ? Are you trapped in a stubborn pattern of sin that you know you're powerless to defeat?

If you continue to try to fight sin and Satan in your own strength, you're only one day closer to the end. There is no reason to continue playing this dangerous game of chess with the devil. You need a substitute. And you have one—Jesus Christ!

Take some time to study the following Scripture passages. Write down the promises they provide and the strategies available to you for confronting Satan. Then bow humbly before the Lord and ask Him to give you victory over Satan by helping you claim and cling to the promises of His Word.

Romans 6:7–11

Promises: _____

_____

_____

Personal Application: _____

_____

_____

Romans 8:1–3, 33–39

Promises: _____

_____

_____

Personal Application: _____

_____

_____

James 4:7

Promises: _____

_____

_____

Personal Application: _____

_____

_____

 Questions for Group Reflection _____

1. How did Jesus' crucifixion and death fulfill the Scriptures? What did his death accomplish as far as the Law was concerned? What was "finished" in His work on the cross?

2. What images from your discussions of Jesus' death have impacted you the most? What have you learned about His character and about the character of God the Father from this chapter?

3. What was significant about Jesus dying as a final sacrifice for our sins? How are His death and resurrection reflected in our corporate worship experiences?

4. In what ways is the story of Christ's death tragic? In what ways is it victorious? Spend some time in prayer meditating on His sacrifice, thanking Him for His love and provision, and worshiping Him.

Chapter 14

"FATHER, INTO YOUR HANDS I COMMIT MY SPIRIT"

Luke 23:44–46

Do you remember making shadow boxes as a child? Our imaginations ran wild as we turned discarded shoeboxes on their sides and transformed them into miniature stages. Creative energy flowed through our fertile minds as we created these tiny cardboard theatres. And best of all, there were no rules! We could depict any scene our minds could imagine, using cotton for clouds and snow, felt strips for grass, and glue sprinkled with sand for the desert. We loved the cramped but captivating world of make-believe.

The stories of Jesus' death recounted by the gospel writers sometimes seem like surreal "shadow boxes" of events that occurred too long ago to imagine. But the crucifixion was *real*. Jesus Christ died that day. His organs shut down systematically. He gasped for His final breath. His lungs collapsed. His heart quit pumping. He *died*.

And just as we learn poignant and powerful lessons from the words Jesus spoke during His perfect earthly life, we learn others from the tender things He said only moments before He died . . . lessons not only on the significance of His death, but also about the life we can have because of it.

The Savior's Final Words

> It was now about the sixth hour, and darkness fell over the whole land until the ninth hour, because the sun was obscured; and the veil of the temple was torn in two. And Jesus, crying out with a loud voice, said, "Father, into Your hands I commit My spirit." Having said this, He breathed His last. (Luke 23:44–46)

Luke, being a physician, was careful to record the final moments of Jesus' life in an accurate historical fashion, much like a CNN reporter framing his evening news bulletin: *The hour is 3:00 P.M., and it's strangely dark. There have been reports of a mysterious tearing of the temple veil in Jerusalem, and Jesus Christ just uttered His last words from the cross: "Father, into Your hands I commit my spirit."*

That was it. Period. No emotional commentary. Only the facts as Luke understood them. But each word of Christ's final cry revealed much about the way He died and the way we should live.

"Father . . ."

Prior to and throughout the long, grueling ordeal of His crucifixion, Jesus remained in constant, close communication with the Father. First, He is depicted somewhere between the upper room and the garden praying, "Father, the hour has come . . . " (John 17). Then from the solitude of Gethsemane, He prayed, "Father, not My will but Yours be done." Hours later, after He'd been nailed to the cross, He petitioned, "Father, forgive them, for they do not know what they are doing." When events climaxed, and He shouldered the weight of our sins, He cried out, "My God, My God, Why have You forsaken Me?"

And here, in the scene Luke describes, Jesus let out His final cry, "Father, into Your hands I commit My spirit." Just before slipping behind death's curtain, Jesus turned to His Father, the eternal God of creation, in prayer. Author Richard Neuhaus notes:

> It is often said that in the intimacy of personal prayer one may address God in many different ways, depending on one's sensibilities and experiences. Perhaps so. The range of the religious imagination should not be unduly shackled, so long as it is not forgotten that the only God we know is the God of Abraham, Isaac and Jacob whom Jesus called "Father." Once again, specificity is all—*this* man, *this* life, *this* death— apart from whom we cannot address God at all. Of course there are many different ideas of God, to which we can apply names that make us, as it is said, "comfortable." But we do not worship an idea of God; we do not pray to an idea of God. As adopted brothers and sisters of Jesus, we pray to His Father who is now our Father.[1]

Hanging in the valley of death's dark shadow, Jesus committed

---

1. Richard John Neuhaus, *Death on a Friday Afternoon: Meditations on the Last Words of Jesus from the Cross* (New York, N.Y.: Basic Books, Perseus Books Group, 2000), p. 231.

His spirit to His heavenly Father, who is light and in whom "there is no darkness at all." (1 John 1:5)

". . . into Your hands . . ."

Jesus prepared for death by acknowledging that His future rested in the Father's hands. However, Acts 2 reveals that Jesus, up to this time, had been captive in the hands of evil men:

> "Men of Israel, listen to these words: Jesus the Nazarene, a man attested to you by God with miracles and wonders and signs which God performed through Him in your midst, just as you yourselves know— this Man, delivered over by the predetermined plan and foreknowledge of God, you nailed to a cross *by the hands of godless men* and put Him to death. But God raised Him up again, putting an end to the agony of death, since it was impossible for Him to be held in its power." (vv. 22–24, emphasis added)

Until He committed Himself to the Father's care, godless men held Jesus captive. As He told His disciples hours before His death, "Behold, the hour is at hand and the Son of Man is being betrayed into the hand of sinners" (Matt. 26:45b).

Sinful hands betrayed Him, bound Him, and led Him away like a stray dog. Sinful hands beat Him and slapped Him in the face. Sinful hands nailed Him to a beam and hoisted Him above the earth. These cruel hands leveled blow after blow of injustice and hate upon the One who had shown them love and mercy.

". . . I commit . . ."

This phrase indicates the *action* of the sentence. In preparation for death's journey, Jesus voluntarily committed His spirit to His Father's care.

But how could this be, if He was bearing the sins of the world? How could Jesus expect such gracious treatment from God, who shortly prior had turned His back on Him? (See Mark 15:34 and Matt. 27:46.) 1 John 2:1–2 provides some perspective:

> My little children, I am writing these things to you so that you may not sin. And if anyone sins, we have an Advocate with the Father, Jesus Christ the righteous; and He Himself is the propitiation for our

sins; and not for ours only, but also for the sins of
the whole world.

When Adam and Eve sinned in the Garden, God's righteous
wrath blazed. The entire human race immediately came under the
condemnation of sin. However, Christ's obedient suffering on the
cross propitiated, or turned away, God's wrath. Christ's death became an acceptable offering that satisfied God's requirements for
righteousness. The price was paid and fellowship was restored.

". . . My spirit."

Jesus' prayer was a tender expression of commitment that He
had most likely learned as a child. His prayer also flows from a
beloved psalm of David:

> Into Your hand I commit my spirit;
> You have ransomed me, O Lord, God of truth.
> (Psalm 31:5)

David's prayer reflected his childlike confidence in the Father's
gracious provision—not only in life, but also in death. Jesus expressed that same confidence in His Father's care only moments
before He died!

After uttering His final words, He was gone. And before the
echo of His cry went silent, the glorious King of heaven slipped
from His battered frame and into His Father's arms. The pain and
suffering ceased. A deafening silence lingered in the air. The execution was over. Christ's death was accomplished . . . and in His
shroud was wrapped the payment for the sins of the entire world.

Martha Snell Nicholson expresses Christ's glorious victory over
death in her poem "The Other Side":

> This isn't death—it's glory!
> It is not dark—it's light!
> It isn't stumbling, groping,
> Or even faith—it's sight!
> This isn't grief—it's having
> My last tear wiped away;
> It's sunrise—it's the morning
> Of my eternal day!
>
> This isn't even praying—
> It's speaking face to face;

Listening and glimpsing
The wonders of His grace.
This is the end of pleading
For strength to bear my pain;
Not even pain's dark memory

Will ever live again.
How did I bear the earth-life
Before I knew this rapture
Of meeting face to face
The One who sought me, saved me,
And kept me by His grace![2]

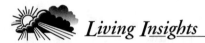 *Living Insights*

Death has been called "the great interrupter," "the grim reaper," "the valley beyond." Or, as Shakespeare's Hamlet mused, "the undiscover'd country from whose bourn / No traveller returns." All of these images focus on the uncertainty, the fearful nature, of death. But because of Christ's triumph, we need not fear death if we know Him as Savior. Rather, as author Erwin Lutzer notes:

> Death, our enemy, can be our friend when God gives us the final call. We can be glad He has given us a shaft of light to illumine the darkness. Death is not a hopeless plunge into the vast unknown.[3]

For Christians, death is not a hopeless plunge. It is the door that leads every believer into the promised presence of the heavenly Father who has prepared a place for us in heaven!

Perhaps a terminal illness has left you or someone you love at death's door. No doubt, fears and questions about the future linger in your mind, even though you are a Christian. You can know the peace of Christ today! As you learn to trust the promises of His Word and meditate on His gracious love and provision for you, He will comfort you with His peace—a peace beyond all understanding.

2. Martha Snell Nicholson, "The Other Side," as quoted by Billy Graham in *Facing Death and the Life After* (Minneapolis, Minn.: Grason Publishing Company, 1987), pp. 232–233.

3. Erwin W. Lutzer, *One Minute After You Die: A Preview of Your Final Destination* (Chicago, Ill.: Moody Press, 1997), p. 13.

Jesus, knowing that God was waiting anxiously to receive Him into heaven, prayerfully committed His soul to His Father's care. And that same assurance of being received into heaven can be yours today.

Take some time to read through the following Scripture passages. As you do, jot down a promise or a word of comfort that can help you or someone you love face death through a peaceful trust in the Lord.

John 11:25

_____

_____

John 14:1–3

_____

_____

1 Corinthians 15:55

_____

_____

2 Corinthians 5:1

_____

_____

2 Corinthians 5:8

_____

_____

Philippians 1:23

_____

_____

Hebrews 2:14–15

_____

1 Peter 1:3–4

 Questions for Group Reflection

1. How would you characterize your current relationship with your earthly father? What was your relationship like as you were growing up? If possible, describe your favorite memory of your father.

2. How would you characterize your current relationship with your heavenly Father? How does your life reflect this relationship? In what ways do your prayers reflect your level of intimacy with God?

3. What do Jesus' prayers tell you about the nature of His relationship with His Father? What does the Father's response tell you about His character? About His love for His Son?

4. How can you demonstrate to others that you are trusting God daily? What practical steps can you take to commit your future to Him? Take time now to pray, releasing your burdens and your future to Him. Ask Him for guidance and direction as you make decisions and seek to follow Him. Turn over your doubts and fears to Him, and ask your Father to comfort you with His peace.

Chapter 15

LESSONS IN OBEDIENCE . . . TAUGHT SEVERELY

Selected Scripture

By now, you may be weary of such focused study on the dreadful suffering Christ endured. We're nearing the end of our discussion of His final dark hours on the cross. But before we step out from under the shadow of the cross, let's linger a bit longer to ask the question, "Can anything valuable come from suffering?"

Clearly, we've established the eternal, incomparable value of Christ's suffering and death in securing our freedom from sin and releasing us from the penalty of death. But what about when we suffer? Can any meaning be found in the pain and adversity that life's inevitable ambushes bring into our lives?

A highly-respected political writer who turned to Christ late in life, Malcolm Muggeridge, expressed that his rockiest roads were often the richest:

> Contrary to what might be expected, I look back on experiences that at the time seemed especially desolating and painful with particular satisfaction. Indeed, I can say with complete truthfulness that everything I learned in my seventy-five years in this world, everything that has truly enhanced and enlightened my existence, has been through affliction and not through happiness, whether pursued or attained. In other words, if it ever were to be possible to eliminate affliction from our earthly existence by means of some drug or other medical mumbo jumbo . . . the result would not be to make life delectable, but to make it too banal and trivial to be endurable. This, of course, is what the Cross signifies.

This chapter has been adapted from "Clearing the Hurdle of Suffering," from the Bible study guide *Clearing the High Hurdles: Overcoming Obstacles to Obeying God's Call,* written by Bryce Klabunde, from the Bible-teaching ministry of Charles R. Swindoll (Anaheim, Calif.: Insight for Living, 1995).

And it is the Cross, more than anything else, that
has called me inexorably to Christ.[1]

When we suffer, we are undeniably linked to Christ and His
cross. God allows suffering in our lives so that we will learn obedience. God's servant Job discovered the importance of following His
commands and trusting His sovereign plan, even in the most dire
circumstances. Job expressed this sentiment in chapter 23:

> He knows the way I take;
> When He has tried me, I shall come forth as gold.
> My foot has held fast to His path;
> I have kept His way and not turned aside.
> I have not departed from the command of His lips;
> I have treasured the words of His mouth more than
> my necessary food. (Job:10–12)

The Psalms also reflect God's purposes for suffering. Psalm 119
states:

> It is good for me that I was afflicted,
> That I may learn Your statutes . . .
> I know, O Lord, that Your judgments are righteous,
> and that in faithfulness You have afflicted me.
> (vv. 71, 75)

In the New Testament, the apostle Paul professes:

> Most gladly, therefore, I will rather boast about my
> weaknesses, so that the power of Christ may dwell
> in me. Therefore I am well content with weaknesses,
> with insults, with distresses, with persecutions, with
> difficulties, for Christ's sake; for when I am weak,
> then I am strong. (2 Cor. 12:9b–10)

Our Savior's journey of obedience led Him down a road of
incredibly severe human suffering. He submitted Himself to the will
of the Father and followed a path that ultimately taught Him to
be obedient unto death—even death on a cross.

---

1. Malcolm Muggeridge, A *Twentieth-Century Testimony* (Nashville, Tenn.: Thomas Nelson
Publishers, 1978).

Lessons Taught Severely

There are several aspects of the person of Christ that we can't identify with. Our words aren't infallible like His. Our works aren't miraculous. Our character isn't perfect. Still, our mutual suffering links our hearts to His on a deeply human level. Think of the events surrounding His death—Jesus was betrayed, beaten, spit on, rejected, cursed, and eventually killed. When we suffer, He understands the depth of our pain.

Jesus also knows firsthand the value of the *process* of learning obedience. The writer to the Hebrews tells us:

> Although He was a Son, He learned obedience from
> the things which He suffered. (Heb. 5:8)

The all-knowing Son of God *learned* something? How can this be? Christ submitted to the Father in perfect obedience, but He had to learn what it was like to obey to the point of suffering. Before He became human, He had never felt pain like we do. It was a new experience for Him—and a necessary one, since He was going to become the High Priest who would mediate between us and the Father.

Because He came to earth, suffered, and died in our place, Jesus has the ability to sympathize with our pain. He viewed suffering and death through human eyes, as the book of Hebrews suggests:

> For we do not have a high priest who cannot sym-
> pathize with our weaknesses, but One who has been
> tempted in all things as we are, yet without sin.
> Therefore, let us draw near with confidence to the
> throne of grace, so that we may receive mercy and
> find grace to help in time of need. (Heb. 4:15–16)

Jesus bore the full weight of our sins as He suffered and died. And because of His triumph over sin, He's there to support us and strengthen us in our times of suffering.

Some Christians believe their lives should be free of pain once Christ takes control. Nothing could be further from the truth! God allows pain and suffering in our lives to deepen our trust in Him. And though, like any loving father, He cares for us deeply and is saddened by our failures and disappointments, He knows that our faith will remain shallow if it is not tested.

The affliction we experience makes our hearts tender, drawing us into a deeper dependence on the Lord. Suffering plants within us the seed of humility, which over time blossoms into obedience. That same obedience bloomed brightly in Christ.

Four Lessons in Obedience

Let's examine four examples of suffering in Jesus' life that taught Him lessons in obedience. Each one is bound to look familiar, for each of us faces these tests at one time or another.

When Suffering Criticism

Jesus learned obedience as He quietly sustained emotional and verbal attacks from others. In John 8, He encountered His most vicious critics, the Pharisees. Jesus' enemies surrounded Him like a pack of hungry jackals as He spoke these words in the temple:

> "I know that you are Abraham's descendants; yet you seek to kill Me, because My word has no place in you. I speak the things which I have seen with My Father; therefore you also do the things which you heard from your father." (vv. 37–38)

"Abraham is our father," the Pharisees snapped back (v. 39a). But Jesus responded:

> "If you are Abraham's children, do the deeds of Abraham. But as it is, you are seeking to kill Me, a man who has told you the truth, which I heard from God; this Abraham did not do." (vv. 39b–40)

Their evil intentions exposed, the Pharisees then took three verbal swipes at Jesus' character. First, they made a vulgar insinuation, suggesting that He was an illegitimate child: "We were not born of fornication" (v. 41). These men knew about Mary's hushed pregnancy and quick marriage to Joseph, and they obviously did not believe that God was Jesus' *true* Father.

In verse 48, the Jewish leaders verbally attacked Him again: "Do we not say rightly that You are a Samaritan and have a demon?" The Samaritans were people with Jewish and Gentile descent, outcasts and half-breeds as far as the Pharisees were concerned. Calling Jesus a Samaritan was meant to cut deeply, but to say He had a demon—that represented the ultimate offense to the Son of God.

The angels in heaven must have yearned to descend in full force against these vile accusers and teach them a lesson or two in kingdom manners. But the one who learned a lesson that day was Jesus. Though he suffered repeated insults, He did not insult back. Instead, He silently and patiently obeyed the Father.

When Suffering Persecution

Jesus also learned obedience through more aggressive acts of persecution by the chief priests and other religious leaders. It wasn't long before their criticism and verbal assaults intensified.

After Jesus brought Lazarus back to life, the Pharisees' murderous desires grew into a detailed plan to get rid of Him (see John 11:47–53). As a result, Jesus limited His movement among them. John 11:54 states:

> Therefore Jesus no longer continued to walk publicly among the Jews, but went away from there to the country near the wilderness, into a city called Ephraim; and there He stayed with the disciples.

The religious leaders issued a warrant for His arrest. And by the time Passover arrived, they had begun enlisting informants:

> Now the chief priests and the Pharisees had given orders that if anyone knew where He was, he was to report it, so that they might seize Him. (v. 57)

It's difficult to imagine the pressure Jesus must have endured. Though hunted like a criminal, forced into hiding, and constantly in danger of being turned over to religious authorities, He knew the secret to remaining calm amid chaos. The hounding, the threats, and the persecution only pressed Him closer to His Father. He clung fiercely to His Father's will and strengthened His resolve to obey.

When Suffering Silence

The third experience of suffering must have been the worst. Jesus learned obedience when God remained silent. It's distressing to hear ugly things said about you. It's frightening to be hunted by persecutors. But nothing compares with the agony of crying out to God and hearing only your own voice echoing in the wind. Jesus' excruciating emotional ordeal in the Garden of Gethsemane reveals the pressure He felt:

> And He came out and proceeded as was His

custom to the Mount of Olives; and the disciples also followed Him. When He arrived at the place, He said to them, "Pray that you may not enter into temptation." And He withdrew from them about a stone's throw, and He knelt down and began to pray, saying, "Father, if you are willing, remove this cup from Me; yet not My will, but Yours be done." Now an angel from heaven appeared to Him, strengthening Him. And being in agony He was praying very fervently; and His sweat became like drops of blood, falling down upon the ground. (Luke 22:39–44)

What sorrow the Father's silence brought to the Savior! Where was God's wonderful plan for Jesus' life? Again and again, Jesus chose to follow the narrow, treacherous path of God's will rather than take the wide, easy road. Through His suffering, He learned to obey, even though the One He followed seemed painfully distant and silent.

When Suffering the Ultimate Wrong

Jesus learned a final lesson of obedience as the wrongs done to Him culminated at the cross. There, all the vulturous evils of hell gathered to devour Christ. Hatred, slander, revenge, cruelty—all raged against Him in a relentless assault on His person, character, and work. Yet the enormous weight of His afflictions did not crush Him. In silent submission, He obeyed to the end.

Final Thoughts

Throughout eternity—past, present, and future—the only time when the Father and Son were separated was when Jesus bore the sins of the world on the cross. Talk about loneliness and agony! Jesus didn't deserve one moment of suffering, yet the apostle Paul wrote:

He made Him who knew no sin to be sin on our behalf, so that we might become the righteousness of God in Him. (2 Cor. 5:21)

By becoming sin for us, Christ identified with our struggles and drew near to us. In turn, our suffering draws us inexorably to Him.

Often we want to live life our way because we think we know best. Then God steps in and says, "Wait a minute. I'm going to have My way in your life. Learn from Me." He allows painful circumstances to deepen our dependence on Him.

We learn to revere lessons taught severely because in the crucible of suffering our character is forged. Our faith is rekindled. And our brokenness makes us more open to our Father's leading.

Living Insights

Philip Yancey wrote these penetrating words about the value of suffering:

> If you once doubt the megaphone value of suffering, visit the intensive-care ward of a hospital. It's unlike any other place in the world. All sorts of people will pace the lobby floors. Some are rich, some poor. There are beautiful, plain, black, white, smart, dull, spiritual, atheistic, white-collar, and blue-collar people. But the intensive-care ward is the one place in the world where none of those divisions makes a speck of difference, for all those people are united by a single, awful thread—their love for a dying relative or friend. You don't see sparks of racial tension there. Economic differences, even religious differences fade away. Often they'll be consoling one another or crying quietly. All are facing the rock-bottom emotions of life, and many of them call for a pastor or priest for the first time ever. Only the megaphone of pain is strong enough to bring these people to their knees and make them reconsider life.[2]

Suffering causes us to reconsider our lives. Our priorities. Our dreams. Our ambitions. In the face of life-shattering events, things that once seemed important to us suddenly appear trivial. Even as our priorities shift due to this "megaphone of suffering," God's still, small voice continues to speak. He says, "You can trust Me. I am near. I will not leave you as you walk through this valley. You are not alone."

When we focus on listening to God's voice in our suffering, we become more intimate with Him. Like trees planted by streams of

---

2. Philip Yancey, *Where Is God When It Hurts?* (Grand Rapids, Mich.: Zondervan Publishing House, 1977), pp. 57–58.

water, as the roots of our faith deepen and take hold in Christ, we grow taller, stronger, and more fruitful.

Ask yourself the following questions:

How have I suffered in the past from the hurtful words or actions of others? Am I currently dealing with a similar situation? How have these experiences affected my life and my spiritual walk?

_____

_____

_____

_____

How have I sensed God's presence during these painful times? If so, how has He manifested Himself?

_____

_____

_____

_____

What steps have I taken to seek out God's will for my life and my situation in those times when He seemed silent?

_____

_____

_____

_____

What lessons have I learned about myself from these painful experiences? How have I matured and grown emotionally? Physically? Spiritually? Relationally?

_____

_____

_____

_____

_____

_____

_____

Perhaps the struggles you named above have been going on for weeks, maybe months, even years. Take a few moments to pray. Address your feelings of frustration, bitterness, and confusion. Tell God honestly how you feel. Then thank Him for lessons taught severely and for the deepening of your trust in Him.

 ## Questions for Group Reflection

1. What is one lesson that you have learned severely? What were the circumstances surrounding the situation? Who was involved? What conclusions did you come to as a result of this event?

2. What are some of the sacrifices that Jesus made in His journey to the cross? What lessons did He learn severely?

3. What have you learned about Jesus through His obedience? What steps do you take in your own life to follow God? What sacrifices have you had to make as a result of following Him?

4. Spend some time in prayer, thanking God for sending His Son to die on the cross for you. Thank Jesus Christ for the sacrifices He made to be obedient unto death and to relate to all of us through His suffering.

Chapter 16

THE DAY GOD ANSWERED, "AMEN"

Selected Scripture

Like others through the centuries who have stood beneath the cross in wonder and amazement, we cannot help but be moved by Jesus' sacrificial act of love. In His life on earth, Jesus spoke on love: "Greater love has no one than this, that one lay down his life for his friends" (John 15:13). In His death, He sealed His sermon with His own blood.

It is possible to examine Christ's death as medical students might examine a patient—scientifically, sanitarily, and detachedly. But as we conclude this first part of our study, let's shed our lab coats and allow the story to penetrate our hearts.

What must those events have looked and felt like? What would it have been like to have been an eyewitness? Or one of Jesus' followers? Let's imagine that we could sit down with someone who had been there and had hoped Jesus would do great things for His people. This follower will share his heart with you. So draw near and listen, because this is his story.

◆

What happened that day is not easy to tell.

I remember that, for the first time since I was a child, I felt afraid of the dark. Something was evil, ominous, about the unnatural blackness that blotted out the midday sun. When the Roman soldiers lit their torches, it was as though the light shone into the darkest pit of hell; and there I saw three men, gasping, bleeding, enveloped in an unholy cacophony of curses and insults.

The nightmarish horror of the crucifixions made me want to run and hide. And yet, at the same time, I felt strangely pulled toward the repulsive scene. For I had met the man in the middle . . . the one called Jesus.

It was years ago, when I first took over my family's business in

This chapter has been adapted from "The Day God Answered, 'Amen,'" from the Bible study guide *His Name Is Wonderful*, by Lee Hough, from the Bible-teaching ministry of Charles R. Swindoll (Anaheim, Calif.: Charles R. Swindoll, Inc., 1992).

Jerusalem. The shop needed some carpentry work, and a friend told me about a father-son business that did a good job for a reasonable price. A deal was struck, and that was when I first met Joseph and his son Jesus.

Many years passed before I was to see Him again. During that time, I became a successful shopkeeper on one of Jerusalem's busiest streets. I loved haggling with people, whether it was over money or the latest gossip. You can imagine how surprised I was when I began hearing about the same carpenter's son who had worked in my shop supposedly changing water into wine and walking on water! And then there was my close friend, Mattathias, who burst into my shop still shaking with the news that he had heard the voice of God saying that Jesus was His Son. "Such nonsense!" I said. "Who could believe it?"

To me, it was just the beginning of another wild rumor about the Messiah. Another imposter claiming to be the Anointed One. No doubt the Romans would kill or scare into silence this would-be Messiah too.

Over the next three years, the stories about Jesus continued to pour into my shop. There were fantastic tales of incredible miracles and tense confrontations with the religious rulers. I never saw the miracles, but I did see the Pharisees, since several of them came by my shop regularly. They were enraged by this "Galilean mountebank," as they called him. Which, by the way, wasn't any worse than some of the things I was told He called them. I sympathized with them; it was bad business to alienate the Pharisees. Still, I didn't really object to the things I heard about Jesus, even though I couldn't bring myself to take much of it seriously. Mostly I tried to stay out of the controversy and just concern myself with business . . . until that one strange, glorious day.

It was the time of Passover, and all week my shop had been brimming with sojourners who had come to celebrate the holy day. But that afternoon, a change suddenly took place in the crowd outside my shop. People were lining both sides of the street, as if expecting to see a passing Roman potentate or a religious parade. Then they began to shout so loudly that I couldn't hear myself talk inside the shop. Everyone hurried outside, including me, and this is what I heard ringing all up and down my street:

"Hosanna!
Blessed is He who comes in the name of the Lord;

133

Blessed is the coming kingdom of our father David;
Hosanna in the highest!"

I quickly threaded my way to the front of the crowd to see what was happening. The shouting became a roar of hysteria as a man riding a donkey approached. People everywhere were throwing tree branches and cloaks onto the road before this peculiar procession of one.

"Who is it?" I shouted to an excited stranger next to me.

"It's the prophet from Nazareth," he cried with tears in his eyes, "the Son of David!" And then he flung his expensive coat into the street just as the lone figure came near.

When I turned to look at the prophet's face, I found Him staring at me. It was Jesus. The boy had become a man, but still I recognized Him. And I think He recognized me too, since He smiled at me with a gentle nod of acquaintance. Just then I felt an arm around my shoulder, and the giant fellow next to me nearly burst my eardrums as he bellowed,

"Blessed is the King who comes in the name of the
Lord;
Peace in heaven and glory in the highest!"

I didn't know what to think or say. All this time I had been hearing about Jesus, He had been just a story to tell, a theory to argue. Now He was real, right in front of me with hundreds, perhaps even thousands, of people heaping praises on him. Children were dancing and cheering in the rain of praise that had completely washed all sadness and despair from the crowd . . . even from me!

"Hosanna to the Son of David, blessed is the King of Israel!" I shouted at the top of my lungs. Me! And it felt wonderful. I couldn't stop shouting and smiling even as the crowd folded in behind Jesus and continued down the street. I just stood there shouting "Hosanna!" lost in a joy I had never felt before.

Finally, the echo of my own voice snapped my reverie, and I noticed Ben Shamon, the shopkeeper across the street, standing there with arms akimbo, staring at me with a look of utter disbelief. Suddenly I felt very foolish and hurried inside.

For the next few days, Jesus took Jerusalem by storm. He threw the greedy money changers out of the temple and thwarted every attempt of the disgruntled Pharisees to discredit Him. Nothing they did could sway the people from hanging on His every word. There were rumors that He was about to establish His rule as the Messiah. It seemed as if the whole city were intoxicated with anticipation, ready to be reborn at Jesus' signal into that golden era of Yahweh's righteous rule. And even though I had chided myself for getting caught up in that scene in the street, I still couldn't deny that I had become intrigued by the Galilean. My cynicism loosened just enough for me to secretly wonder, *Could He really be the one?*

Then it happened. I had just entered my shop early one morning when Diosthenes appeared. He was the Greek who owned the tent shop next door. His visits were rare, and even more rarely did he have anything good to say.

"Greetings, Diosthenes," I said.

"Well, they got Him."

"I'm fine, thank you. And you?"

"It was one of His own."

"Wait . . . what are you talking about?"

"You know, the Galilean, the one who's been parading around talking as if He were a god Himself. They arrested Him last night after one of His disciples turned Him in."

"What? Are you sure it was Jesus?"

"Absolutely. They caught Him hiding right there in Gethsemane. I heard that when they tried to arrest Him, He started a scuffle and cut off some poor fellow's ear. They finally had to tie Him up."

"What have they done with Him?"

"My cousin says He's been on trial all night long because the chief priests and Pharisees are in a hurry to get Him crucified."

Crucified. The word struck me like a stone. Diosthenes left, and my thoughts reeled from the awful impact of his news. Was Jesus a hoax, just another pretender out to con everyone? At first my head pounded with furious anger. I wanted to forget that He ever existed, that I had ever shouted "Hosanna" or held the slightest hope that He might have been the Messiah. "He deserves to be crucified," I tried to convince myself. But the words were hollow. They weren't really what was in my heart. But why would Jesus allow all this to happen if He truly was the Messiah?

"Lord, what's happening?" I prayed. "Is He . . . no, it's impossible!" I could not believe or disbelieve. Hours later, the only thing I felt I could do, must do, was go see Him at the place where criminals were crucified. Skull Hill.

As I arrived, the Roman soldiers were pounding the spikes into the hands and feet of not one, but three convicted men. Agonizing cries of tortured men mingled with the wails of inconsolable women. I felt unnerved and sickened by the sounds. When they lifted up the crosses, the crowd began brutally tearing at Jesus with their taunts, like jackals moving in for the kill. "He saved others, but He can't save Himself! . . . Save Yourself; come down from the cross, if You are the Son of God!"

I couldn't bring myself to draw too close. And even though I could tell which one was Jesus by the way they taunted Him, I couldn't recognize Him physically. They had beaten Him too badly for that.

Then the midday darkness came. Night swallowed up the sun, sky, trees, hill, people, crosses; everything was erased into one vast oblivion. An eerie silence ensued in that nothingness, punctuated only by the pained gasps of the dying.

The soldiers quickly lit torches. The crowd seemed nervous, afraid. But then someone cursed the Nazarene, blaming Him for this bad omen. A second voice agreed, and a third, and slowly you could sense the fear release itself in mockings that grew bolder and more hateful under the cover of darkness.

Enough! I thought. I wanted to leave, to run from this frightful obscenity. But as in a boyhood nightmare, I couldn't move my legs. I stood transfixed by the horrible sight. Minutes passed . . . hours . . . and suddenly Jesus hurled a wail of chilling despair into the blackness.

"Eloi, Eloi, lama sabachthani?"

The man next to me thought he was calling for Elijah. "No," I whispered, "He calls God." And I remember shuddering as I translated Jesus' desperate words aloud. "My God, My God, why have you abandoned me?"

What did this mean? If He was the Messiah, why had God now abandoned Him? My mind whirled when the man beside me asked, "Did you hear about the suicide last night?"

"No."

"One of His disciples hung himself. He's been abandoned all right, by both God and that ignorant rabble He called His disciples. I heard that every one of them deserted Him. I knew He wasn't Messiah. Messiahs don't reign from bloody crosses, do they?" and he grinned.

I turned in disgust and immediately noticed a hyssop branch with a sponge on it being lifted up to Jesus. I moved closer to see what was happening. Again, Jesus spoke with a loud voice, "It is finished!" Incredibly, He said it as one would shout for joy at a victory just won. What victory? And then he said, in a final thunderous cry, "Father, into Your hands I commit My spirit," and it was over. He was dead, and I felt completely undone and confused.

I began to weep. Then suddenly I felt the earth shudder and begin to shake uncontrollably as if it, too, were in anguish over His death. People started running in every direction, fleeing, falling, yelling for help. Huge rocks split apart, hurling fragments into the terrified crowd. Everyone was afraid, including an awestruck Roman centurion who said, "Truly, this was the Son of God!"

Son of God? Messiah? For the next two days and into the early morning hours of the Sabbath, I could hardly sleep; I was so haunted by that horrible event. Was Jesus the Messiah? Why did God forsake Him? What did He finish? "Great Adonai," I pled, "who was that man in the middle?"

Then I remembered something my friend Mattathias had said the day he rushed into my shop with the news about God naming Jesus as His Son. He had also related how the prophet John the Baptist had pointed at Jesus and said, "Behold, the Lamb of God who takes away the sin of the world!"

Lamb . . . lamb. I had seen thousands offered on the temple altar as the sacrificial atonement for our sins. Blood was shed and— wait, that was it! That's what Jesus' crucifixion was all about. Why hadn't I understood this before? Jesus was God's human lamb, a sinless sacrifice. What was it that the rabbi had read last Saturday?

> He was oppressed and He was afflicted,
> Yet He did not open His mouth;
> Like a lamb that is led to slaughter,
> And like a sheep that is silent before its shearers,
> So He did not open His mouth. (Isa. 53:7)

Yes, that was it. But there was more.

> Surely our griefs He Himself bore,
> And our sorrows He carried;
> Yet we ourselves esteemed Him stricken,
> Smitten of God, and afflicted.
> But He was pierced through for our transgressions.
> He was crushed for our iniquities;
> The chastening for our well-being fell upon Him,

And by His scourging we are healed.
All of us like sheep have gone astray,
Each of us has turned to his own way;
But the Lord has caused the iniquity of us all
To fall on Him. (vv. 4–6).

No sooner had I begun to grasp these truths than the house began to shake in a second violent earthquake. It was only later that I learned it was caused by the angel who descended that morning and rolled away the stone from Jesus' grave. To me it was like God saying, "Amen" to His Son's victory cry of "It is finished!" Jesus *is* the Messiah.

And He is risen!

 Living Insights

Before you go back to your life-as-usual routines, consider an important question posed by Max Lucado in his poignant book *No Wonder They Call Him the Savior.*

> The immensity of the Nazarene's execution makes it impossible to ignore . . . Everybody has an opinion. Everyone is choosing a side. You can't be neutral on an issue like this one. Apathy? Not this time. It's one side or the other. All have to choose.
>
> And choose they did.
>
> For every cunning Caiaphas there was a daring Nicodemus. For every cynical Herod there was a questioning Pilate. For every pot-mouthed thief there was a truth-seeking one. For every turncoat Judas there was a faithful John.
>
> There was something about the crucifixion that made every witness either step toward it or away from it. It simultaneously compelled and repelled.
>
> And today, two thousand years later, the same is true. It's the watershed. It's the Continental Divide. It's Normandy. And you are either on one side or the other. A choice is demanded. We can do what we want with the cross. We can examine its history. We can study its theology. We can reflect upon its

prophecies. Yet the one thing we can't do is walk away in neutral. No fence sitting is permitted. The cross, in its absurd splendor, doesn't allow that. That is one luxury that God, in his awful mercy, doesn't permit.

On which side are you?[1]

Would you take a moment to consider this question? Perhaps you've come this far and still are unsure. Won't you come over to the side of faith in Christ, the side of a personal relationship with the One who died for you? If that is your desire, here's a simple prayer you can use to express your faith:

Dear God,

I know that my sin has put a barrier between You and me. Thank You for sending Jesus to die in my place. I accept Your gift of eternal life and ask Jesus to be my personal Savior. Please begin to guide my life. Thank You. In Jesus' name I pray. Amen.

If you've prayed this prayer and you wish to find out more about knowing God and His plan for you in the Bible, contact us at Insight for Living. You can speak to one of our pastors on staff by calling (972) 473-5097. Or you can write to us at Insight for Living, Pastoral Ministries Department, Post Office Box 269000, Plano, Texas, 75026.

You may have already made the choice of faith in Christ. If so, in the space provided, perhaps you would like to affirm your commitment in prayer. Write out the feelings in your heart as one standing beneath the cross. Let the Savior know of your love for Him.

_____

_____

_____

_____

_____

---

1. Max Lucado, *No Wonder They Call Him the Savior* (Portland, Ore.: Multnomah Press, 1986), pp. 72–73.

_____

_____

_____

_____

_____

_____

_____

_____

_____

 Questions for Group Reflection

1. Richard John Neuhaus, in his book *Death on a Friday Afternoon*, writes: "Every day of the year is a good day to think more deeply about Good Friday, for Good Friday is the drama of the love by which our every day is sustained."[2] What does this mean to you?

2. As you reflect on all that you've learned about Christ's sacrificial death on the cross, what has impacted you most? What would you like to learn more about?

3. What difference has what you've learned about Jesus made in the way you live?

4. Draw near to one another now and pray that you would each be rooted more deeply in God's great, steadfast love for you. And remember in prayer those who haven't accepted God's love for them yet, and ask the Lord how you could help express that love to them.

2. Richard John Neuhaus, *Death on a Friday Afternoon: Meditations on the Last Words of Jesus from the Cross* (New York, N.Y.: Perseus Books Group, Basic Books, 2000), p. ix.

PART TWO

THE DAWN

"Through the heartfelt mercies of our God,
  God's Sunrise will break in upon us,
Shining on those in the darkness,
  those sitting in the shadow of death,
Then showing us the way, one foot at a time,
  down the path of peace."
(Luke 1:78–79 THE MESSAGE)

The dawn. Dramatic streaks of crimson and yellow against a canvas of clouds signal the end of night and the beginning of day. Spiritually speaking, the dawn is a metaphor for new life—new creation—in Christ, where the dark shadow of death that shrouds our lives is forever chased away.

According to Scripture, before Christ came we were all "sitting" in death's darkness, because what else could we do? We frail humans couldn't stand against death; neither could we run from its grip. So we sat and waited and watched for a glimmer of hope on the horizon. Then came Christ—the Son and Sunrise of God—who defeated death by dying for our sins and rising from the grave (1 Cor. 15:3, 21–22, 54b–56).

Death no longer has the last word; instead, Life now has the final say!

What does Jesus' resurrection accomplish? It vindicates Christ's name—all He ever said and did is proved true. It validates His death as being effective for forgiving sins. It enables believers, through His Spirit, to live in power over sin. It assures us of our future resurrection, when we will always be with Him. And it gives us a present, living hope. Just as dawn pushes back the darkness, so Jesus' resurrection disperses our despair.

Some may follow a dead hero into death, but only a living Savior can usher us into life. Only Jesus can guide us through the darkness into the dawn.

Chapter 17

WHAT IS YOUR VERDICT?

Selected Scripture

Jesus' work on the cross set in place the great theological corner-stones of Christianity: *redemption, justification, reconciliation, forgiveness.* But without Jesus' resurrection, these stones would be lost in the tangled weeds of an abandoned lot. If Jesus' body had remained in death's grip, sin would still have its choke hold on our souls. The apostle Paul explained:

> If Christ has not been raised, your faith is worthless; you are still in your sins. Then those also who have fallen asleep in Christ have perished. If we have hoped in Christ in this life only, we are of all men most to be pitied. (1 Cor. 15:17–19)

Thankfully, Christ is risen! Because He defeated death to live anew, we know that He truly was the Son of God who atoned for our sins and now enables us to live in His resurrection power. And because the Father raised His Son from the grave, we know He will raise us as well. Our hope rests in a *living* Savior.

Skeptics, of course, cast doubt on the biblical accounts of the Resurrection. Like prosecutors in a courtroom, they accuse the gospel writers of twisting the "real" story to serve their own purposes. They admit that Jesus' tomb is empty, but they offer alternative theories to explain why His body is missing.

For the next few moments, let's enter the courtroom of ideas and, as members of the jury, hear the arguments for and against the Resurrection. Remember, more than a historical event is on trial here. At stake is the foundation of our hope, the very heart of our Christian faith. Are you ready to hear the case?

Then let's begin. Court is in session.

Three Alternative Theories to the Resurrection

First to approach the jury is the prosecutor who seeks to dismantle Christianity by attacking it at its core. With an air of confidence in his voice, the prosecutor offers three possible theories to explain the disappearance of Jesus's body.

The swoon theory. This theory claims that, instead of dying on

145

the cross, Jesus "swooned" into a coma. Everyone at the scene assumed He was dead, and they removed His body and buried Him. The coolness of the tomb revived Him, though, and He slipped into the night, appearing before His followers who supposed that He was raised from the dead. This theory asserts that Christianity is based on a mistake.

The kidnap theory. According to this explanation, Jesus died on the cross and was buried just as the gospel writers say. However, determined to keep Jesus' religious movement alive, some daring disciples tiptoed past the guards, pushed back the stone, and stole His body. Where they hid it, no one knows. They spread the resurrection rumor, and within a generation, Christianity had spread around the world. According to this theory, the entire religion is based on a lie.

The hallucination theory. What about the testimonies of the disciples who claimed to see their resurrected Lord? The prosecutor offers this explanation: the intensity of grief over Jesus' death caused the disciples to *think* they saw Jesus. In other words, they hallucinated. In a state of emotional fervor, their minds played tricks on them. As a result, they truly believed Jesus had been raised from the dead, and they passed their stories to other disciples, who believed them as fact. This theory says Christianity was founded by people who had been duped.

Bringing his argument to a dramatic climax, the prosecutor pauses to let his points settle into the jurors' minds. Now his challenge rests squarely on the shoulders of the defense: "Prove beyond a reasonable doubt that Jesus rose from the dead!"

The Truth about Jesus' Death

The defense first calls to the witness stand the gospel writers, who testify that Jesus died, not swooned, on the cross. Matthew states that Jesus "yielded up His spirit" (27:50); Mark, that He "breathed His last" (15:37); Luke, that "He breathed His last" (23:46); and John, that He "gave up His spirit" (19:30). Their records indicate that Jesus was in control even of His final breath. At the moment of His own choosing, Jesus yielded Himself to death.

The Roman soldiers at the scene also testify. The centurion who oversaw the crucifixion detail was standing right in front of Jesus when He died. This seasoned veteran of many bloody battles had seen the ghastly face of death in many men's eyes. In Jesus' eyes, however, he beheld the face of God:

> When the centurion, who was standing right in front of Him, saw the way He breathed His last, he said, "Truly this man *was* the Son of God!" (Mark 15:39, emphasis added)

Don't overlook the past tense *was*. He believed Jesus was dead, and later he reported that fact to Pilate (vv. 44–45).

The other soldiers at the scene pronounced Jesus dead as well. They had been ordered to break the legs of the three crucified victims in order to hasten their deaths. They did so to the criminals on either side of Jesus, but "when they saw that He was already dead, they did not break His legs" (John 19:33). Instead:

> One of the soldiers pierced His side with a spear, and immediately blood and water came out. (v. 34)

Water probably refers to the whitish serum that, at death, collects in the pericardium, the membrane surrounding the heart. The spear punctured the membrane and the heart itself, causing the blood in the inner chamber and the watery serum to flow together from His side—a sign of certain death.

Two other men take the stand next: Joseph of Arimathea and Nicodemus. Members of the ruling religious council that condemned Jesus, these two secret followers of His came out of the shadows to give Jesus a proper burial (vv. 38–39). They couldn't stop their own countrymen from crucifying Jesus like a criminal, but they could make certain that He was buried like a king.

Nicodemus carried with him a hundred pounds of burial spices—an extravagant amount befitting a royal funeral. As was the Jewish custom, he and Joseph wrapped the body in linen, sealing the strips with a thick, cement-like plaster of spices to mask the smell of the decaying body (see vv. 39–40).

The wrappings hardened to form a body cast that left only the face uncovered. A linen cloth was then placed over the face. Had the two friends noticed the faintest breath in Jesus' lungs, surely they would have tried to revive Him. Yet there was no life in Him; their Master was dead.

Could Jesus have swooned on the cross and then, in His weakened condition, escaped both the linen cocoon and the tomb? Hardly. But what about the other theories? Could the disciples have stolen the body?

The Truth about Jesus' Resurrection

The answer comes through an analysis of the scene at the tomb. Joseph of Arimathea offered to lay Jesus' body in his own tomb because it was near the crucifixion site (v. 41a). Two important facts are given: first, it was a "new tomb"—Jesus' body was the only body in the tomb (v. 41b); second, it "had been hewn out in the rock"—there was only one way in and one way out (Mark 15:46).

The Displaced Stone

Joseph probably placed the body on a shelf carved out of the wall of the tomb, then rolled a large stone in front of the entrance to protect the body from grave robbers and roaming animals (Matt. 27:60). The heavy stone, perhaps weighing a ton or more, was likely set at an incline and wedged in place with a piece of wood, called a chock. By removing it, one man could let gravity roll the stone in place, but it would take many men to roll it back.

As the stone shut tight the entrance to the tomb, Joseph and Nicodemus' solemn task was complete. They hurried home because the sun was setting and the Sabbath was at hand. As devout Jews, they wanted to purify themselves to celebrate the holy day.

The next morning the chief priests and Pharisees—the rival parties that had conspired to kill the upstart Nazarene—collaborated one more time to make certain that Jesus' religious revolution stayed buried with His body. Together, they approached Pilate with a request:

> "Sir, we remember that when He was still alive that deceiver said, 'After three days I am to rise again.' Therefore, give orders for the grave to be made secure until the third day, otherwise His disciples may come and steal Him away and say to the people, 'He has risen from the dead,' and the last deception will be worse than the first." Pilate said to them, "You have a guard; go, make it as secure as you know how." And they went and made the grave secure, and along with the guard they set a seal on the stone. (Matt. 27:63–66).

The Jewish leaders anticipated the "kidnap" scenario, and they determined to turn the tomb into a maximum security prison cell. Jesus' unarmed disciples would be unable to overpower a guard of battle-trained Roman soldiers, and any individuals caught breaking a Roman seal would be hunted down and punished by death. The tomb was sealed as tightly as humanly possible; Jesus' body was locked away, and the Jewish leaders' problem was solved . . . or so they thought.

In a paradoxical twist, the Jewish leaders' security measures only added proof to the Resurrection. Early Sunday morning several women came to anoint Jesus' body with more spices. They wondered, "Who will roll away the stone for us from the entrance of the tomb?" (Mark 16:3). But when they arrived, "The stone had been rolled away, although it was extremely large" (v. 4). Who could have fought past the guards, dared to break the Roman seal, and heaved back the stone?[1] No human!

According to Matthew's account, an angel moved the stone:

> And behold, a severe earthquake had occurred, for an angel of the Lord descended from heaven and came and rolled away the stone and sat upon it. And his appearance was like lightning, and his clothing as white as snow. The guards shook for fear of him and became like dead men. (Matt. 28:2–4)

This magnificent heavenly creature rolled away the stone—not to let Jesus out, but to allow people *in*. In His resurrected form, Jesus had already passed through the tomb walls. So the angel invited the women in:

> "Do not be afraid; for I know that you are looking for Jesus who has been crucified. He is not here, for He has risen, just as He said. Come, see the place where He was lying. Go quickly and tell His disciples that He has risen from the dead; and behold, He is going ahead of you into Galilee, there you will see Him; behold, I have told you."
> And they left the tomb quickly with fear and great joy and ran to report it to His disciples. (vv. 5–8)

---

1. "The verb John uses is not the one we would expect for rolling a stone . . . it means rather something like 'lift up.' It seems as though John means us to understand that the stone was lifted out of its groove. What had taken place was no ordinary phenomenon, but the result of an exercise of divine power." Leon Morris, *Reflections on the Gospel of John: Crucified and Risen,* John 17–21 (Grand Rapids, Mich.: Baker Book House, 1988), vol. 4, p. 688.

The burial methods, the sealed tomb, the Roman guard, the earthquake, the angel, and finally the displaced stone all prove that the Resurrection is true. But there's more. How do we explain the missing body?

The Empty Tomb

On the way to the tomb, the women had wondered how they would roll away the stone to anoint Jesus' body; now they were wondering, "Where *is* Jesus' body?"

Only three possible answers explain the disappearance of Jesus' body. First, *Jesus awoke from His "swoon" and left under His own strength.* As we've seen, Jesus was dead. But suppose He had been barely alive. Can you imagine Him staggering to the tomb door, gripping the inside edges of the huge stone, and rolling it up the incline by Himself? Impossible.

Second, *someone stole His body and hid it.* But who? Only two groups could have done such a thing—either Jesus' enemies or His friends. If His enemies removed the body, surely they would have produced it when the disciples later proclaimed, "He is risen!" However, the Jewish leaders never played this trump card. They never used the greatest argument against Christianity—the body of Jesus—because they didn't have it and didn't know where it was.

Perhaps, then, Jesus' friends stole His body. As you recall, the Jewish leaders feared the disciples would do just that. Ironically, now that the tomb was empty, the Jewish leaders bribed the guards to spread this story:

> And when they had assembled with the elders and
> consulted together, they gave a large sum of money
> to the soldiers, and said, "You are to say, 'His disciples
> came by night and stole Him away while we were
> asleep.' And if this should come to the governor's
> ears, we will win him over and keep you out of
> trouble." And they took the money and did as they
> had been instructed; and this story was widely spread
> among the Jews, and is to this day. (vv. 12–15)

Because no one would have believed that the disciples subdued the Roman guard, the elders told the soldiers to say that they fell asleep on duty while the disciples made off with the body. How likely was it, though, that *all* the soldiers fell asleep and *none* awakened at the sound of the disciples heaving back the stone and fumbling in the darkness?

And how likely was it that these soldiers would doze off in the first place, knowing that the punishment for sleeping on duty was death?

And how likely was it that the beaten down and leaderless disciples, who had not yet understood the meaning of the Resurrection (see John 20:9–10), would even concoct such a plan?

And how likely was it that after supposedly stealing the body, the disciples would later sacrifice their lives as martyrs for a cause they knew was based on a hoax?

The elders had to lay a lot of "grease" on the soldiers' palms to convince them to spread this ridiculous lie. Despite the gaping holes, though, the story spread among the Jews.

Jesus' enemies didn't take His body; Jesus' friends couldn't have stolen it. The only possible explanation for the missing body: resurrection.

The Grave Clothes

We say the tomb was empty, but in reality it contained one key item: the linen grave clothes. According to John's account, Mary Magdalene frantically reported the missing body to Peter and John: "They have taken away the Lord out of the tomb, and we do not know where they have laid Him" (John 20:2). The two disciples ran to the grave site, assuming it was a crime scene:

> The two were running together; and the other disciple [John] ran ahead faster than Peter and came to the tomb first; and stooping and looking in, he saw the linen wrappings lying there; but he did not go in. And so Simon Peter also came, following him, and entered the tomb; and he saw the linen wrappings lying there, and the face-cloth which had been on His head, not lying with the linen wrappings, but rolled up in a place by itself. So the other disciple who had first come to the tomb then also entered, and he saw and believed. (vv. 4–8)

At first, Peter and John were puzzled. If thieves stole the body, wouldn't they have taken the grave clothes too? Why leave them behind? And how could they have slipped the body out of the tightly wrapped linens, leaving the body's shape still in them? It didn't make sense!

In those brief moments in the tomb, the truth began to dawn in the two disciples' hearts. As John recorded the account, he used three different Greek words for the word *saw* to mark a progression of insight.[2] In verse 5, the Greek term for *saw* is *blepei*.[3] It basically means "to see" and carries a strong "emphasis on the function of the eye."[4] John peered into the cave and noticed the linen wrappings, but their significance did not immediately hit him.

Next came Simon Peter, puffing up behind John. Shouldering past John into the tomb, he "saw" what John had seen but in a different way. The Greek word used here is *theorei*,[5] from which we get our word *theorize*. Peter saw something he wasn't expecting, and it stopped him in his tracks. Eyes narrowed, brow furrowed, he studied it and pondered what it could mean.

Peter could not figure it out, but John was beginning to. Verse 8 records the third Greek word: John "saw and believed." This time the word *saw, eiden* in Greek,[6] means "to perceive," "to realize."[7] In other words, it all fell into place; it clicked. John stood next to Peter gazing at that odd sight, and the light came on. "Peter, Peter, He's been raised from the dead! He's alive!" John may not have understood Jesus' resurrection as foretold by Scripture (v. 9), but what he saw, he believed.

In the days that followed, John's seeing-and-believing experience repeated itself in the lives of a growing circle of people who saw Jesus alive. The two men traveling to Emmaus saw and believed when they recognized that the stranger with them was Jesus Himself (Luke 24:13–35). Jesus' disciples saw and believed when their

2. Portions of the remainder of this chapter have been adapted from the study guide *The Majesty of God's Son*, written by Jason Shepherd, from the Bible-teaching ministry of Charles R. Swindoll (Anaheim, Calif.: Insight for Living, 1999), pp. 131–32.

3. See Edwin A. Blum, "John," in *The Bible Knowledge Commentary*, New Testament edition, ed. John F. Walvoord and Roy B. Zuck (Colorado Springs, Colo.: Chariot Victor Publishing, 1983), p. 342.

4. Gerhard Kittle and Gerhard Friedrich, eds., *Theological Dictionary of the New Testament*, translated and abridged in one volume by Geoffrey W. Bromiley (1985; reprint, Grand Rapids, Mich.: William B. Eerdmans Publishing Co., 1992), p. 706.

5. See Blum, "John," p. 342.

6. See Blum, "John," p. 342.

7. Kittle and Friedrich, eds., *Theological Dictionary of the New Testament*, p. 710.

Master appeared in their midst (vv. 36–53). And, according to Paul, that was just the beginning of the long line of eyewitnesses who saw and believed:

> He appeared to Cephas, then to the twelve. After that He appeared to more than five hundred brethren at one time, most of whom remain until now, but some have fallen asleep; then He appeared to James, then to all the apostles; and last of all, as to one untimely born, He appeared to me also. (1 Cor. 15:5–8)

The Defense Rests

Ladies and gentlemen of the jury, the evidence has been presented and the witnesses have told their stories. The defense rests . . . but the verdict remains undecided. Did Jesus rise from the dead? Can He, as a living Savior, offer real hope for this life and the life to come?

Throughout history, many of those who have heard the case have believed the evidence, but perhaps for you the issue remains unresolved. Christ won't force your vote before you're ready. He is patient. But still He needs to know . . . your verdict, please.

 Living Insights

The early disciples didn't believe the Resurrection until they saw Jesus alive. And doubting Thomas refused to believe until he saw Jesus face-to-face and touched the imprint of His wounds (see John 20:19–28). The old saying, "Seeing is believing," was certainly true for Thomas, as it might have been for us if we were in his sandals.

Believing in the Resurrection without seeing Jesus alive is perhaps the ultimate faith challenge. Jesus acknowledged its difficulty when He commented to Thomas after appearing before him:

> "Because you have seen Me, have you believed? Blessed are they who did not see, and yet believed." (v. 29)

Believing without seeing calls upon a higher level of faith, but it yields a greater spiritual blessing. And it almost always is the result of a journey.

Where are you in your faith journey? Do you see yourself more as a doubting Thomas or a believing Thomas . . . or somewhere in between?

_____

_____

_____

For many of us, faith grows with facts. Frank Morison is an interesting example of a man who found his faith in the facts of the Resurrection. Here's a bit of his story.

Frank Morison was a well-educated British lawyer, his thinking shaped by the German critics, Oxford professor Matthew Arnold, and biologist Dr. Thomas Huxley—all of whom openly denied even the possibility of miracles.

Morison, in an effort to disprove the Christian belief that Jesus was miraculously raised from the dead, set out to write a book. Little did he suspect that the book he ended up writing would be so radically different from the book he had planned. _Who Moved the Stone?_ turned out to be a defense of the bodily resurrection of Christ. In his own words, he "discovered one day that not only could he no longer write the book as he had once conceived it, but that he would not if he could."[8] And this change of heart happened "not suddenly, as in a flash of insight or inspiration, but slowly, almost imperceptibly, by the very stubbornness of the facts themselves."[9]

Can you identify with Morison's feelings about the "stubbornness" of the facts? Which facts about the Resurrection that we studied in this lesson have stubbornly planted themselves in your mind?

_____

_____

_____

_____

_____

8. Frank Morison, _Who Moved the Stone?_ (Grand Rapids, Mich.: Zondervan Publishing House, Lamplighter Books, 1958), preface.

9. Morison, _Who Moved the Stone?_, preface.

How have these facts encouraged your faith?

_____

_____

_____

_____

Through the remainder of this study, we'll expose various nuances of the Resurrection, and hopefully, you'll feel your faith grow. Take a few moments at this point to thank the Lord for the evidences of the Resurrection that we find in Scripture. In the space provided, reaffirm your commitment to the journey, and ask for His grace to deepen your faith along the way.

_____

_____

_____

_____

Questions for Group Reflection

1. Some people believe that the Christian life is a matter of faith only—that we shouldn't need "proof" to convince us that Christ is real and what He said is true. In light of our study of the gospel writers' accounts of Jesus' resurrection, what do you believe is the relationship between faith and facts? Does God offer us proof about Himself? What would that be?

2. Imagine that we didn't have such convincing proof. What would your life look like without an Easter Sunday?

3. What gives you the most hope about Jesus' empty tomb?

4. Aren't you glad you have a living, life-giving, present Lord who rules in love? Join together to give Him your collective praise, thanking Him for being a Light that no amount of darkness can ever put out!

Chapter 18

A SUNDAY MORNING MIRACLE

Mark 16:1–3, 10–14; John 20:1–18

"Believe in God, believe also in Me." (John 14:1b)

Jesus invited people to believe in Him. Not just in His teaching. Not just in His cause. Not just in His ideology. But in *Him*.

He called people to a personal faith—faith in a Person. Plenty of traveling rabbis plied the dusty Judean landscape urging people to believe their way. But only Jesus peered into the searching eyes of suffering people and said, "*I* am the way" (John 14:6, emphasis added). Only Jesus announced to those stumbling in sin's darkness, "*I* am the Light of the world" (9:5, emphasis added). And only Jesus said to those streaming through the gates of traditional religion in an effort to find God, "*I* am the door; if anyone enters through Me, he will be saved" (10:9, emphasis added).

In response to His intensely personal call, many of His followers sacrificed everything in devotion to Him. Into His outstretched arms they cast their families and futures, their hopes and dreams. These were the men who, for His sake, left their fishing nets and their careers on the shores of the Sea of Galilee. These were the women whose tears of adoration stained His feet. These were the ones whose worlds shattered when He died.

The Roman soldiers who drove the nails into Jesus' hands and feet might as well have driven them straight into His disciples' chests. Their life's hope drained from their hearts with every drop of blood from Jesus' veins. And when He breathed His last, a part of them died with Him.

They had believed in Him, as He had asked. And now, not only was their Master dead, His body was gone! At the tomb, Peter and John saw nothing that remained of the One who held their lives in His hands—nothing except linen rags.

Parts of this chapter have been adapted from "Reactions to the Resurrected Lord," from the study guide *Exalting Christ . . . The Lamb of God*, rev. ed., written by Wendy Peterson, from the Bible-teaching ministry of Charles R. Swindoll (Anaheim, Calif.: Insight for Living, 2000).

The two pondered what they saw and believed something miraculous had happened. But many baffling questions lingered in their minds:

> "For as yet they did not understand the Scripture,
> that He must rise again from the dead" (John 20:9).

A lone figure in the shadows also did not yet understand the Scripture—a woman weeping as though her whole world had been shattered, and shattered again.

The Empty Tomb

An empty tomb. This is all Mary Magdalene saw. This is all she understood.

Her Lord, who had freed her from the living death of being possessed by seven demons (see Luke 8:2), had been betrayed and brutalized, murdered and entombed. And now He couldn't even rest in peace. Her mind couldn't conceive of resurrection, only grave robbery. Some mysterious "they" had taken Him out of the tomb, and she didn't know where He was (John 20:2).

Had the Jewish leaders decided that the disgrace of crucifixion was not enough? Had they stolen His body in order to strip Jesus of every shred of dignity?

For Mary, they stole so much more than Jesus' body. They deprived her of the comfort of tenderly anointing Him in death. Now she couldn't say her final good-bye. He was gone, desecrated, nowhere to be found. Tears of anger and grief, frustration and helplessness poured out in sobs.

However, Jesus—who is always near His brokenhearted children—was nearer to Mary than she knew.

Jesus Appears to Mary

Troubled and confused, Mary wept so much that she didn't see the miracle in front of her, didn't seem to realize that she was talking with angels:

> But Mary was standing outside the tomb weeping; and so, as she wept, she stooped and looked into the tomb; and she saw two angels in white sitting, one at the head and one at the feet, where the body of Jesus had been lying. And they said to her, "Woman,

why are you weeping?" She said to them, "Because they have taken away my Lord, and I do not know where they have laid Him. (John 20:11–13)

Maybe it was hazy or foggy that morning . . . maybe tears blurred her eyes . . . maybe Jesus was the last person she expected to see. But when she turned around, she didn't recognize the One for whom her heart was aching.

When she had said this, she turned around and saw Jesus standing there, and did not know that it was Jesus. Jesus said to her, "Woman, why are you weeping? Whom are you seeking?" Supposing Him to be the gardener, she said to Him, "Sir, if you have carried Him away, tell me where you have laid Him, and I will take Him away." (vv. 14–15)

Jesus kindly repeated the question the angels asked, "Woman, why are you weeping?" Through the teary haze of her pain, Mary could only see what she had lost. Mary wept as if her life had come to an end. The empty tomb, however, signified that Mary's new life in Christ was just beginning.

Aren't we like Mary sometimes? The pain of loss limits our perspective so we can't see beyond our own empty hands. While we weep, the Lord stands right next to us with arms outstretched, ready to offer us the hope of His presence. He offered Himself to Mary, but she still didn't recognize His voice. But when He called her by name, He came immediately into focus:

Jesus said to her, "Mary!" She turned and said to Him in Hebrew, "Rabboni!" (which means, Teacher). (v. 16)

Although not explicitly stated, the next verse implies that Mary, overcome with joy, fell at Jesus' feet and clung to Him for all she was worth. Tears of joy replaced sobs of sorrow, and she determined to never let Him go again.

Gently but firmly, Jesus urged her to release Him. He was establishing a whole new relationship with His followers, one based not on touch and sight but on faith. After His ascension, Mary would receive more than the comfort of His physical presence; He would send the Holy Spirit to His followers, and they would possess the power of His spiritual presence within them (see John 16:7–14).

Besides, others were still mourning and needed to hear the good news. So Jesus bestowed on Mary the privilege of telling the disciples that He was alive!

> Jesus said to her, "Stop clinging to Me, for I have not yet ascended to the Father; but go to My brethren and say to them, 'I ascend to My Father and your Father, and My God and your God.'" (20:17)

Did you notice the subtle shift in Jesus' choice of words? In the Upper Room, He had called His disciples His friends (15:15). Now they are His brothers; sharing the same Father, they had "become children of God" (1:12). And this new relationship, made possible by Jesus' resurrection, is available to all who believe in Him. Her heart overflowing with joy, Mary ran to do as her Lord had asked:

> Mary Magdalene came, announcing to the disciples, "I have seen the Lord," and that He had said these things to her. (20:18)

Jesus Appears to the Disciples

How did Jesus' tightest circle of followers receive the news of His resurrection? Turn to Mark's gospel to find out how the disciples reacted to Mary's breathless announcement.

The Disciples' Initial Unbelief

> She went and reported to those who had been with Him, while they were mourning and weeping. When they heard that He was alive and had been seen by her, they refused to believe it. (Mark 16:10–11)

The other disciples refused to believe, even though Peter and John had seen the evidence and Mary had seen the resurrected Lord. Why? What held them back?

If you've ever had your heart broken, if your dreams have ever come to a disastrous end, maybe you can understand the disciples' hesitancy. Did they dare raise their hopes only to risk being disappointed again? Hadn't they put their hearts on the line once already, only to have them crushed? It was too much to ask for them to trust again.

Even after hearing that Jesus appeared to two others, whom Luke identified as the two men walking from Jerusalem to Emmaus (see

Luke 24:13–35), the other disciples still couldn't bring themselves to believe (Mark 16:12–13). So high were their protective walls that only a personal appearance from Jesus Himself could tear them down:

> Afterward He appeared to the eleven themselves as they were reclining at the table; and He reproached them for their unbelief and hardness of heart, because they had not believed those who had seen Him after He had risen. (v. 14)

The disciples' self-protection had hardened into unbelief . . . and the same can happen to us, particularly after a traumatic event. Too much caution can calcify our hearts, drawing us inward so that we think only of ourselves: our pain, our disappointment, our security. It took Jesus' reproach, like a chisel, to break through the disciples' self-focused fear and release their faith. Sometimes it takes a stern confrontation to shake us out of our self-pity and get our eyes back on the Lord.

The Disciples' Eventual Transformation

But Jesus had more to say to His trembling disciples than words of reproach. In John's account, we hear His gentle reassurance:

> So when it was evening on that day, the first day of the week, and when the doors were shut where the disciples were, for fear of the Jews, Jesus came and stood in their midst and said to them, "Peace be with you." (John 20:19)

The disciples expected to hear at the door the banging of a Roman sword seeking their blood. Instead, they heard the voice of their dead Master, a sound that terrified them even more! *Ghost!* was their first thought, but with Jesus' greeting, "Peace be with you," a calm settled over their hearts, and they gathered the courage to come near:

> And when He had said this, He showed them both His hands and His side. The disciples then rejoiced when they saw the Lord. So Jesus said to them again, "Peace be with you; as the Father has sent Me, I also send you." And when He had said this, He breathed on them and said to them, "Receive the Holy Spirit. If you forgive the sins of any, their sins have been

forgiven them; if you retain the sins of any, they have been retained." (John 20:20–23)[1]

As the Father sent Jesus to show and tell the world of God's redeeming love, so now Jesus commissions His disciples to go and do the same. He breathes on them the Spirit (which will later indwell them fully at Pentecost [see Acts 2]).[2]

The church's mission is to proclaim the forgiveness of sins that Christ has *already* won. Jesus has provided forgiveness of sins to all who believe in Him, but those who do not will remain in their sins. The apostle Paul later summed up the church's assignment:

> God . . . reconciled us to Himself through Christ and gave us the ministry of reconciliation . . . We are ambassadors for Christ. (2 Cor. 5:18b, 20a)

Before Christ's appearance, the disciples were not the most likely ambassadors. Aimless and disillusioned, they were afraid to leave their locked room. Even their boldest leader, Peter, had turned coward when he denied Christ three times the night of the arrest.

In the weeks and months after Jesus appeared, however, these same men and women went out proclaiming the message of Christ to great crowds, suffering imprisonment, beating, and even martyrdom for their relentless testimonies. What transformed these timid sheep into roaring lions? The same life-changing resurrection power that is available to us today.

> Christ came back from the dead so we might live as He lived and claim the triumph He has provided. He didn't die just to be studied and oohhed and aahhed over; He died and rose again to offer, through His blood and His life, new life—transforming power

1. This passage has led some to conclude that God authorizes certain Christians to declare people forgiven or not forgiven. The Greek text says, "He breathed on," excluding the word *them*, implying that Jesus aimed His action toward the whole group, not individuals. Commentator Leon Morris makes a broader, more accurate application of Jesus' action: "The gift of which he is about to speak is a gift made to the church rather than to individual members." Leon Morris, *Reflections on the Gospel of John: Crucified and Risen*, John 17–21 (Grand Rapids, Mich.: Baker Book House, 1988), vol. 4, p. 709.

2. "We should perhaps bear in mind that in Greek the word we translate 'Spirit' also means 'breath' or 'wind.' It was thus very appropriate that Jesus should use breath as an outward sign of the gift of the Spirit that he was giving the disciples." Morris, *Reflections on the Gospel of John*, p. 710.

to live beyond the dregs of depravity's leftovers. And the first evidence we see of this is in the lives of Jesus' once frightened and disillusioned followers.[3]

The Power of Belief

At the crucifixion, the skies went black as if the sun had blinked out of existence. For the disciples, the sun might as well have been extinguished because the Light of their lives had died. But, at the Resurrection, a new day of hope dawned. Jesus was alive! By raising Him, God raised up the disciples. Jesus comforted them with peace, guaranteed them an inheritance with Him in heaven, and filled them with the same grave-bursting power God displayed in Him (see Eph. 1:18–20).

The Sunday morning miracle started a chain reaction of transformation in the disciples that will spread to all those who believe Jesus' wonderful message. Because Jesus lives, we live too. Death no longer masters our destiny. Fear no longer holds us captive. Through Christ's eyes, we can see beyond our graves to our own resurrection Sunday. The Son has risen! Hallelujah!

 *Living Insights*

It is a popular practice these days to choose our religion like we might shop for clothes. We stroll through the mall of ideas, window-shopping the world religions. We may try on a spiritual practice from the Buddhism rack. Or we may mix and match a few ideas from Hinduism and humanism. This belief fits our lifestyle, so we toss it in our bag. That belief is too confining, so we put it back. Like consumers, we go picking and choosing through the religions, taking or leaving whatever we like.

If Jesus had not been raised, Christianity might have been just another shop in the mall, just another rack of nice ideals to pursue for our religious wardrobe. "Love you neighbor." "Love your enemy." "Love everyone."

The Resurrection, however, puts Christianity in a separate category. Buddha, Muhammad, Confucius, Aristotle—all the religious

3. Charles R. Swindoll, *The Darkness and the Dawn* (Nashville, Tenn.: Word Publishing, 2001), p. 263.

leaders and philosophers of the world remain in their tombs; but Jesus' grave is empty. And that fact changes everything.

In his book *The Jesus I Never Knew*, Philip Yancey describes the unique challenge of the Resurrection:

> In many respects I would find an unresurrected Jesus easier to accept. Easter makes him dangerous. Because of Easter I have to listen to his extravagant claims and can no longer pick and choose from his sayings. Moreover, Easter means he must be loose out there somewhere. Like the disciples, I never know where Jesus might turn up, how he might speak to me, what he might ask of me.[4]

Our world seems determined to line up Jesus alongside all the other religious teachers, to give Him only a spot in history and a holiday on the calendar—essentially, to put Him back in His grave. A vital part of our journey of faith is confessing the uniqueness of Jesus and holding on to that confession with all we've got.

Perhaps you need to take a moment to prayerfully reexamine your faith. What do you believe about Jesus' resurrection?

_____

_____

_____

_____

How does the Resurrection reaffirm your faith in God? His power? His love? His forgiveness?

_____

_____

_____

Fear was the first reaction of those who saw Jesus alive, yet not one of the disciples fled from Him. Instead, they drew near to Him. Draw near to the Lord in prayer as you conclude this section. Thank

---

4. Philip Yancey, *The Jesus I Never Knew* (Grand Rapids, Mich.: Zondervan Publishing House, 1995), pp. 225–26.

Him for His appearances to Mary and the disciples. Invite Him to reveal Himself once more through your hands of service as you love others in His name.

_____

_____

_____

_____

_____

 Questions for Group Reflection

1. As a group, brainstorm on some of the spiritual realities Jesus' resurrection has brought about. For example, what does the empty tomb say to those who put Christ on the cross?

2. What has Jesus' resurrection meant to you personally—what difference has it made in your life? Has it:

   • made you more hopeful when you go through hard times?

   • given you a strong sense of meaning and purpose?

   • comforted you when grief has wrung your heart?

   What else can you add to this list?

3. One of the things Jesus wants His resurrection to give us is peace. He repeatedly told His disciples, "Peace be with you" (John 20:19, 21, 26). Yet in a world like ours (and theirs)—filled with hatred, violence, war, terrorism, poverty, and death—fear comes more naturally than peace, doesn't it? Good has not yet completely overcome evil, light has not yet over-taken darkness, love has not yet overcome hate, and life has not yet displaced death—not yet. But that time is coming! Jesus' resurrection is a kind of down payment that God's purpose will be fulfilled.

   How do we live in the meantime, though? How do we not let our hearts be troubled but set them securely in the peace Jesus gives us (read John 14:27; 16:33; Rom. 8:6; 16:20)? How can we cultivate an Easter perspective in a Good Friday kind of world?

4. "Where two or three have gathered in My name, I am there in their midst," Jesus tells us (Matt. 18:20). As He was with His disciples, so Jesus is now in your midst. Bring to Him the troubles of your heart, the fears, the griefs, even the doubts. Ask Him to make His presence more real to you, to give you joy and strength for your sorrow and fear. And ask that you may experience His peace more fully.

 Digging Deeper

Jesus' appearance to Mary Magdalene and the disciples were just two of at least thirteen occasions in which Jesus revealed Himself after the Resurrection. But it can be difficult to reconcile the various accounts. Bible scholar J. Oswald Sanders pieced together Christ's appearances in the following order:

> To Mary Magdalene (John 20:14–16; Mark 16:9–11)
> To other women [Mary, the mother of James,
> Salome, and Joanna (Mark 16:1; Luke 24:10)]
> (Matthew 28:8–10)
> To Peter (Luke 24:34; 1 Corinthians 15:5)
> To the Emmaus disciples (Like 24:13–31;
> Mark 16:12–13)
> To the ten [excluding Thomas] (Luke 24:36;
> John 20:19)
> To the eleven [including Thomas] (Mark 16:4;
> John 20:26; 1 Corinthians 15:5)
> To the seven [at the Sea of Tiberias] (John 21:1–14)
> On the Galilee mountain (Matthew 28:16–17;
> Mark 16:15–18; 1 Corinthians 15:6)
> To the five hundred (1 Corinthians 15:6)
> To James (1 Corinthians 15:7)
> At the Ascension (Luke 24:44–53; Mark 16:19–20;
> Acts 1:6–11)
> To Stephen (Acts 7:56)
> To Paul (1 Corinthians 15:8)[5]

5. J. Oswald Sanders, *The Incomparable Christ*, rev. and enl. ed. (1952; reprint, Chicago, Ill.: Moody Press, 1971), pp. 215–16.

Chapter 19

CURING THE
PLAGUE OF DEATH

Ecclesiastes 3; Romans 5:6–21

The Black Plague that infected London in the seventeenth century crept into the city quietly, claiming only a few lives in early 1664. A year later, 590 deaths had been reported. By June of 1665, the number had swelled to 6,137. Panic raged through the streets of London as the death toll reached 17,000 in July. In August of the same year, terrified Londoners fled the city as the number of deaths soared to a staggering 31,000. But the nightmare had only begun. By the time the plague peaked, the bodies of more than 70,000 men, women, and children had been buried or burned.

What caused this catastrophe? The infinitesimal bites of fleas carried by diseased rats. Sadly, people thought that bad-smelling air caused the sickness, so they carried sweet-scented posy petals in their pockets in hopes of warding off the disease. Hospitals even walked victims through fragrant rose gardens in an effort to rid their lungs of the dreaded illness. The superstitious rite cured no one, of course. It's said that one man sang these haunting words as he piled the corpses of countless victims onto his cart for delivery to the mass graves:

> Ring around the roses,
> A pocket full of posies;
> Ashes, ashes, we all fall down.[1]

Ironically, children around the world sing this parody of calamity as an innocent nursery rhyme. Yet for those who know the horror of its history, the last line soberly reminds us of the greatest plague of all—death.

This chapter has been adapted from "Curing the Plague of Death," in the Bible study guide *Shedding Light on Our Dark Side*, written by Lee Hough, from the Bible-teaching ministry of Charles R. Swindoll (Anaheim, Calif.: Charles R. Swindoll, Inc., 1993).

1. As told by Charles R. Swindoll in *Come Before Winter . . . and Share My Hope* (Portland, Ore.: Multnomah Press, 1985), p. 34.

"Death is a debt we all must pay," wrote the Greek poet Euripides.[2] Even those fortunate enough to escape London's horrible plague died eventually. No matter what we do to delay or deny death, eventually we will all fall down, just as the nursery rhyme says.

Physical death is part of the curse God placed upon humanity as a result of Adam and Eve's disobedience in the Garden of Eden. The following Scripture passages attest to this grim truth:

> By the sweat of your face
> You will eat bread,
> Till you return to the ground,
> Because from it you were taken;
> For you are dust,
> And to dust you shall return. (Gen. 3:19)

> What man can live and not see death?
> Can he deliver his soul from the power of Sheol?
> (Ps. 89:48)

> It is appointed for men to die once and after this comes judgment. (Heb. 9:27)

> Yet you do not know what your life will be like tomorrow. You are just a vapor that appears for a little while and then vanishes away. (James 4:14)

It's clear from these passages that learning to face death is a natural part of living in a fallen world. Even believers struggle with the uncertainty of what lies ahead. Our faith in God guides us, but we don't have all the answers. In this chapter we will examine some ways of understanding and coping with death and take steps towards coming to terms with our own mortality. And, more importantly, we will discover God's wonderful and fulfilling purposes for us in life!

Examination: Cures in Contrast

Despite death's obvious and inevitable reality, most of us struggle to accept our own mortality. Over the centuries, many philosophies have been prescribed to help people cope with death. King Solomon, the writer of Ecclesiastes, lists six philosophies that he tried—all of which failed to offer him true fulfillment and peace.

---

2. Euripides, as quoted in *The Home Book of Quotations*, 10th ed., comp. Burton Stevenson (New York, N.Y.: Dodd, Mead, and Co., 1967), p. 377.

Human Philosophies

Fatalism (Eccl. 3:1–9). This bleak belief is often called the "doctrine of despair." It teaches that events are fixed in advance for all time and follow a blind, irrational process that leaves humankind without meaning, responsibility, or significance.

Skepticism (vv. 10–11). The skeptic believes that nothing can be known for certain. The central theme behind this way of thinking is that man will not find out the work that God has done. According to this philosophy, everything we believe to be true is suspect. Doubt is a way of life. The pinnacle of skepticism is *agnosticism*, the theory that God is unknowable and inexpressible.

Hedonism (vv. 12–13). The followers of this lifestyle devote themselves to the pursuit of personal pleasure. They believe in no life after death and no punishment for sins, so they live for today and don't worry about the future. "Eat, drink, and be merry, for tomorrow we may die" is their guiding principle (see 1 Cor. 15:32).

Deism (vv. 14–17). Adherents of deism believe that God created the world to run according to natural laws and without His supernatural interference. This concept denies the possibility of miracles, including the greatest one of all—God becoming flesh in Christ to offer Himself up as the sacrifice for our sins.

Evolutionism (vv. 18–19). This philosophy, championed by Charles Darwin, suggests that God did not create man in His image. Rather, it teaches that we are all simply animals that evolved from prehistoric, primordial slime. Chance and change rule our fate as we strive for "the survival of the fittest." According to evolutionism, this life is all there is; death ends everything.

Universalism (vv. 20–22). According to this philosophy, we "all go to the same place." Universalists believe that everyone is intimately connected with the "universal soul" and that all people will be resurrected to live happily ever after in heaven with God. No need to worry about sin, judgment, or hell. Here, all people have the promise of paradise.

Proverbs 14:12 says, "There is a way which seems right to a man, But its end is the way of death." Each of the above philosophies has seemed plausible and palatable to people throughout the ages. But none proved any more effective in curing the plague of death than posy petals did in curing the Black Plague.

The Divine Remedy

In contrast to these humanistic elixirs, God's Word offers a sure remedy for the plague of death. Let's turn to Romans 5 and read the apostle Paul's words regarding our desperate condition and God's sure remedy.

The truth. Beginning in verse 12, we're given a brief case history of death:

> Therefore, just as through one man sin entered into the world, and death through sin, and so death spread to all men, because all sinned.

The plague originated with Adam's disobedience. The immediate result was that "sin entered into the world," and the ultimate end was that, like a plague, "death spread to all."

The formula. We could take the truths of this verse and translate them into this simple formula:

Humanity + Iniquity = Depravity

Depravity places all of us "under sin" (Gal. 3:22). And that puts us in the worst possible position before a holy God. This same truth is underscored by our desperate condition. Paul used three other terms in this chapter to describe the unsaved: "helpless" (Rom. 5:6), "sinners" (v. 8), and "enemies" (v. 10). Together, these paint a bleak portrait of humanity helplessly afflicted by sin.

The hope. Mercifully, Christ provided a cure that delivered us from the ultimate penalty of sin—eternal separation from God through death (Eph. 2:4). Romans 5:17–21 stakes a powerful claim against death's ravages:

> For if by the transgression of the one, death reigned through the one, much more those who receive the abundance of grace and of the gift of righteousness will reign in life through the One, Jesus Christ.
>
> So then as through one transgression there resulted condemnation to all men, even so through one act of righteousness there resulted justification of life to all men. For as through one man's disobedience the many were made sinners, even so through the obedience of the One the many will be made righteous. The Law came in so that the transgression would increase; but where sin increased, grace

abounded all the more, so that, as sin reigned in death, even so grace would reign through righteousness to eternal life through Jesus Christ our Lord.

Jesus Christ cured the plague of death by victoriously overcoming the grave.

What assurance do we have that Christ's remedy for death works? An empty tomb! Muhammad's grave is occupied. So is Buddha's. Even Abraham's body is still buried somewhere in the land of promise. But Christ's tomb is empty—and death is swallowed up in victory! Paul rejoices over this incredible truth in his first letter to the Corinthians:

> But now Christ has been raised from the dead, the first fruits of those who are asleep. For since by a man came death, by a man also came the resurrection of the dead. For as in Adam all die, so also in Christ all will be made alive. (1 Cor. 15:20–22)

Sadly, rose beds and posy petals never cured anyone. Only Jesus, the risen Savior, has overcome death's plague, trading a tired, powerless superstition for a glorious confession of faith! Now, Christians are able to proclaim this wondrous truth:

> I will sing of my Redeemer
> And His wondrous love to me;
>
> On the cruel cross He suffered
> From the curse to set me free.
>
> Sing, O sing of my Redeemer,
> With His blood He purchased me;
>
> On the cross He sealed my pardon
> Paid the debt and made me free![3]

---

3. "I Will Sing of My Redeemer," in *Hymns for the Family of God* (Nashville, Tenn.: Paragon Associates, Inc., 1976), pp. 228–29.

Are you haunted by a nagging fear of dying? Are you uncertain about what lies ahead for you? God wants to grant you peace of mind about your future. By claiming Christ as your Savior, you can be delivered from the plague of death.

All of us will die a physical death, but Christ has freed us from the penalty of spiritual death, which would separate us from God forever. And we know that freedom the moment we place our trust in Christ by faith.

Christians need not fear death's appointment. God has made a way for us to have eternal life through Christ. The sting has been removed from death. The grave knows no victory. The hope of life eternal has been ushered in through Christ's triumphant death.

Ruth Bell Graham expressed in these poignant verses her hope of life beyond the grave:

> When death comes
> will it come quietly
> —one may say creep—
> as after a hard
> and tiring day, one lies
> and longs for sleep—
> ending age and sorrow
> or youth and pain?
> Who dies in Christ
> has all to gain
> —and a Tomorrow!
> Why weep?
> Death may be a savage.
> We cannot be sure:
> the godly may be slaughtered,
> evil men endure;
> however death may strike,
> or whom,
> who knows the risen Lord
> knows, too, the empty tomb.[4]

---

4. Ruth Bell Graham as quoted by Billy Graham in *Facing Death and the Life After* (Minneapolis, Minn.: Grason Publishers, 1987), p. 139.

Questions for Group Reflection

1. Have you lost any close friends or family members during your lifetime? If so, how have these losses affected you? In what ways has losing a loved one made you think about your own mortality?

2. What differing philosophies of life and death have you encountered? In what ways have you seen people living according to the human philosophies described by King Solomon (fatalism, skepticism, hedonism, deism, evolutionism, universalism)? How do you explain and display your Christian understanding of the meaning of life to others?

3. How is death portrayed in your culture? What aspects of it seem to be emphasized by the media? What metaphors do we use to refer to death? How does this differ from what the Bible says about life and death in Christ?

4. Explain the ways in which Christ conquered death. Then, spend some time in prayer, remembering the suffering He experienced out of His great love and compassion for you. Praise Him for His victory over death and the grave, and thank Him for the promise of abundant and eternal life in Him.

Chapter 20

BREAKING DEATH'S JAWS
Selected Scripture

Woody Allen once quipped, "It's not that I'm afraid to die, I just don't want to be there when it happens"![1]

Humor helps us cope with our fears about death, but we all know only too well that death is no laughing matter. We dread the pain of loss and the absence of the people we love. And taking that final journey into the unknown ourselves is something most of us are afraid to even talk about.

The worst thing about death is that there's no escape from it. After Adam sinned, the Lord told him, "For you are dust, / And to dust you shall return" (Gen. 3:19b). Every human being since has faced the same fate. Other Scriptures reiterate our earthly destiny:

> What man can live and not see death?
> Can he deliver his soul from the power of Sheol?
> (Ps. 89:48)

> "The person who sins will die." (Ezek. 18:20a)

> Through one man sin entered into the world, and death through sin, and so death spread to all men, because all sinned. (Rom. 5:12)

> For as in Adam all die . . . (1 Cor. 15:22a)

Though many people view death by suicide as a painless escape from the realities of life, it is no guaranteed end to misery. Death opens the door to eternity—one marked by joyful communion with the Lord for those who belong to Christ . . . or one of endless torture for any person who dies without Him.

Since we cannot escape death, we must face it with courage and faith. To do that, we need the divine perspective found in the pages of God's Word. John 11 provides not only theological insights into death's relentless assault on humanity but also a hope-filled illustration of Christ's power to break its merciless hold.

---

1. Woody Allen, "Death (A Play)," in *Without Feathers* (New York, N.Y.: Random House, 1975), p. 99.

The Illness of Lazarus

A short distance east of Jerusalem lay a tiny hamlet called Bethany, home to Lazarus and his two sisters, Martha and Mary, who were all close friends of the Savior. When Jesus was exhausted by the strain of public ministry, He sometimes retreated to this familiar Judean town and found renewal in the company of this family. To be sure, they enjoyed a rare, intimate relationship with the Teacher from Galilee.

However, all was not peaceful in Bethany at this particular time. Lazarus lay deathly ill, while his sisters anxiously kept watch at his bedside (John 11:1–2). In desperation and hope, Martha and Mary sent word to their Master and Friend:

> "Lord, behold, he whom You love is sick." (v. 3)

The Response of Jesus

Jesus' response at first seems puzzling:

> But when Jesus heard this, He said, "This sickness is not to end in death, but for the glory of God, so that the Son of God may be glorified by it." Now Jesus loved Martha and her sister and Lazarus. So when He heard that he was sick, He then stayed two days longer in the place where He was. (vv. 4–6)

Two days? If He loved them, why didn't He rush to their aid? Well, He *did* love them, but He also had a divine mission. As He told His disciples, He—as God's means of salvation for the world—had to be glorified and bring glory to God for the Father's saving work through Him (v. 4). Jesus also needed to give His disciples one more sign so they would believe in Him and continue His ministry after Him (v. 15).

In order to accomplish this twofold task, Jesus had to risk His own life:

> Then after this, He said to the disciples, "Let us go to Judea again." The disciples said to Him, "Rabbi, the Jews were just now seeking to stone You, and are You going there again?" (vv. 7–8)

Jesus replied that while He still had time on this earth, He would use it to do God's work (vv. 9–10). Part of that work was to wait two days. But what exactly was Jesus waiting for? He explained to His disciples:

> "Our friend Lazarus has fallen asleep; but I go, so that I may awaken him out of sleep." (v. 11)

Interpreting this literally, the disciples replied, "Lord, if he has fallen asleep, he will recover" (v. 12). So Jesus put it plainly:

> "Lazarus is dead . . . let us go to him" (vv. 14–15b).

Jesus waited in order to allow death to come to someone He loved. Lazarus' illness and death became a crucial juncture in Jesus' life. After the miracle He was about to perform in Bethany, His own journey turned hard into the shadow of the cross. Lesslie Newbigin explains how this miracle, the last of Jesus' seven signs,[2] foretold the life-giving power of His own death:

> This miracle most fitly concludes the series of signs and forms the transition to the story of the passion. . . . It shows that Jesus gives life only by giving his life. The raising of Lazarus leads directly to the death of Jesus. It is at the cost of life that he gives life. The "abundant life" that he gives is life through death.[3]

Against the dark backdrop of Lazarus' sickness and death, the light of God's glory would shine brightly. Who could have known that out of all this bleakness would come a ray of life-giving hope?

The Reactions of Martha and Mary

By the time Jesus reached Bethany, Lazarus had been in the tomb for four days (v. 17).[4] Jesus' late arrival sparked significant

---

2. John records seven signs or miracles that testify to Jesus' being the Son of God come to bring salvation to the world: His changing water into wine at Cana (2:1–11); healing the government official's son with just His word (4:46–54); healing the man lame for thirty-eight years at Bethesda (5:1–18); feeding the five thousand (6:1–13); walking on water (vv. 16–21); restoring sight to the man born blind (9:1–7); and raising Lazarus from the dead (11:1–44).

3. Lesslie Newbigin, *The Light Has Come: An Exposition of the Fourth Gospel* (Grand Rapids, Mich.: William B. Eerdmans Publishing Co., 1982), p. 138.

4. "Lazarus must have died shortly after the messengers left Bethany, accounting for the 'four days' of vv. 17, 39: one day for the journey of the messengers, the two days when Jesus remained where he was, and a day for Jesus' journey to Bethany." Leon Morris, note on John 11:4, in *The NIV Study Bible*, ed. Kenneth L. Barker (Grand Rapids, Mich.: Zondervan Bible Publishers, 1985), p. 1618. It was Jewish custom to bury a person's body the day he or she died.

reactions in Martha and Mary:

> Martha therefore, when she heard that Jesus was coming, went to meet Him, but Mary stayed at the house. (v. 20)

A woman of action, Martha took the initiative to speak with Jesus, still hoping that He might be able to do something—although what that would be she didn't know:

> Martha then said to Jesus, "Lord, if You had been here, my brother would not have died. Even now I know that whatever You ask of God, God will give You." (vv. 21–22)

Hurting and confused, Martha nevertheless affirmed her faith in Jesus as God's Son. In response, Jesus moved to comfort her with the miracle He would soon bring about.

> "Your brother will rise again." (v. 23b)

Thinking that these familiar words referred to the final resurrection,[5] Martha responded:

> "I know that he will rise again in the resurrection on the last day." (v. 24)

Jesus, however, brought God's powerful presence up close, radically transforming her understanding of life and death with His next self-revealing words:

> "I am the resurrection and the life; he who believes in Me will live even if he dies, and everyone who lives and believes in Me will never die. Do you believe this? (vv. 25–26)

"*I* am the resurrection; *I* am life—*I* am the future you hope for here in the present," Jesus told her. Martha had hoped for her brother's healing, but:

> healing can only help us so far; it does not solve the problem of death. The answer to death is not healing

---

5. Martha "shared with Jesus and with Pharisaic Judaism a belief in the resurrection, a view roundly denied by the Sadducees (Mark 12:18–27; Acts 23:8)." D. A. Carson, *The Gospel according to John* (Grand Rapids, Mich.: William B. Eerdmans Publishing Co., 1991), p. 412.

but resurrection.

. . . The promise of the resurrection is fulfilled in the coming of Jesus. Faith in him gives life now and the promise of life after death. The resurrection life, as verses 25 and 26 spell out, begins with faith and is not destroyed by the death of the body.[6]

"Do you believe in this, Martha? Do you believe in Me?" Jesus was trying to get Martha to see that "resurrection is no longer a mere doctrine: it has a living face and a name. Jesus is himself the presence of the life which is God's gift beyond death."[7]

Was the light of Jesus' presence enough to dispel death's darkness and set Martha's faith ablaze? The Lord must have delighted to hear her answer:

"Yes, Lord; I have believed that You are the Christ, the Son of God, even He who comes into the world." (John 11:27)

Martha needed her faith expanded, but her more sensitive and introspective sister needed her broken heart pieced back together with infinite tenderness:

When she [Martha] had said this, she went away and called Mary her sister, saying secretly, "The Teacher is here and is calling for you." And when she heard it, she got up quickly and was coming to Him.

Now Jesus had not yet come into the village, but was still in the place where Martha met Him. Then the Jews who were with her in the house, and consoling her, when they saw that Mary got up quickly and went out, they followed her, supposing that she was going to the tomb to weep there. Therefore, when Mary came where Jesus was, she saw Him, and fell at His feet, saying to Him, "Lord, if You had been here, my brother would not have died." (vv. 28–32)

6. R. Wade Paschal, Jr., "The Message of John," in *The Bible for Everyday Life* (Oxford, England: Lion Publishing, 1988; reprint; Grand Rapids, Mich.: William B. Eerdmans Publishing Co., 1988), p. 210.

7. Newbigin, *The Light Has Come*, p. 142.

Though He was the Giver and Sustainer of life, Christ's heart broke at the thought of Lazarus' death and the sight of Mary's raw grief. John tells us:

> When Jesus therefore saw her weeping, and the Jews who came with her also weeping, He was deeply moved in spirit and was troubled, and said, "Where have you laid him?" They said to Him, "Lord, come and see." Jesus wept. (vv. 33–36)

Still trembling, Jesus made His way to the tomb—that stone testament of creation gone awry. What happened next proved that even the cold, hard ground of death's tomb was no match for the Creator of every living thing.

The Raising of Lazarus

> So Jesus, again being deeply moved within, came to the tomb. Now it was a cave, and a stone was lying against it. Jesus said, "Remove the stone." Martha, the sister of the deceased, said to Him, "Lord, by this time there will be a stench, for he has been dead four days." Jesus said to her, "Did I not say to you that if you believe, you will see the glory of God?" So they removed the stone. Then Jesus raised His eyes, and said, "Father, I thank You that You have heard Me. I knew that You always hear Me; but because of the people standing around I said it, so that they may believe that You sent Me." (vv. 38–42)

In His prayer, Jesus reiterated the ultimate purpose of the miracle He had come to Earth to perform. His Father's glory would be revealed and others would believe that God loved the world so much that He sent His only Son to save any who would believe. Then Jesus turned His gaze toward the tomb and

> cried out with a loud voice, "Lazarus, come forth." The man who had died came forth, bound hand and foot with wrappings, and his face was wrapped around with a cloth. Jesus said to them, "Unbind him, and let him go." (vv. 43b–44)

John wrote simply, "The man who had died came forth." We can only imagine the scene. Grieving friends and family members stood stunned in disbelief as Lazarus came stumbling into the sunlight. He had been dead and in the cave four days. Jesus said, "Come out!" and immediately death released its jaws and let its prey go. Lazarus lived again!

The Ultimate Triumph

There will come a day, according to the Scriptures, when this same Giver of life will call forth the dead from their graves, just as He did with Lazarus. Burial plots around the world will split open and give up their dead. Paul wrote about this very day in 1 Corinthians 15:

> Now I say this, brethren, that flesh and blood cannot inherit the kingdom of God; nor does the perishable inherit the imperishable. Behold, I tell you a mystery; we will not all sleep, but we will all be changed, in a moment, in the twinkling of an eye, at the last trumpet; for the trumpet will sound, and the dead will be raised imperishable, and we will be changed. For this perishable must put on the imperishable, and this mortal must put on immortality. But when this perishable will have put on the imperishable, and this mortal will have put on immortality, then will come about the saying that is written: "Death is swallowed up in victory. O Death, where is your victory? O death, where is your sting?" The sting of death is sin, and the power of sin is the law; but thanks be to God, who gives us the victory through our Lord Jesus Christ. (vv. 50–57)

That about covers it, doesn't it? Death will one day no longer reign over our mortal bodies. Though Lazarus was raised from the dead, he died again. But someday he, too, will be raised to live forever as his mortal body becomes immortal, his perishable frame, imperishable. And so it shall be for all who know Christ as Lord and Savior. He has given us the victory over the grave. He is the resurrection and the life. Believe in Him, and though you will die, you will live!

Author Joseph Bayly wrote these pointed words on the subject of death:

> Death always waits. The door of the hearse is never closed.
>
> Dairy farmer and sales executive live in death's shadow, with Nobel prize winner and prostitute, mother, infant, teen, old man. The hearse stands waiting for the surgeon who transplants a heart as well as the hopeful recipient, for the funeral director as well as the corpse he manipulates.
>
> Death spares none.[8]

All this talk of hearses and corpses would keep us awake at night were it not for the promise of resurrection. That is what the story of Lazarus provides for us: a genuine hope beyond the grave. Yet there's more. Our hope is not merely in a future theological reality. Our hope is in Jesus Himself, our Savior, our God, and our Friend. Do you believe that today?

Maybe you or someone you love is facing death even as you read these words. Perhaps your family continues to reassemble the pieces of a life that was shattered by the death of a loved one. Reflect on the comforting truths we've studied in this story.

How would you describe your feelings about death? Does it frighten you? Are you confused by conflicting perspectives on the afterlife? Explain.

_____

_____

_____

_____

_____

_____

8. Joseph Bayly, *The Last Thing We Talk About*, rev. ed. (Elgin, Ill.: David C. Cook Publishing Co., 1973), pp. 11–12.

Has the study of Lazarus's death and resurrection calmed your anxieties and fears about death? How?

_____

_____

_____

_____

How does seeing Jesus weep help you walk through your valley of grief? What particular part of this story touched you personally? Why did it touch you so?

_____

_____

_____

_____

_____

Jesus longs for you to turn to Him. To trust His power. To receive His grace. That's especially true in times when life seems senseless and we question His care. Are you burdened deeply today? Turn to the Savior. He will meet you as He did Martha and Mary, offering to comfort your hurting soul.

 Questions for Group Reflection

1. For some of us, even when an astounding miracle happens right in front of our faces, we still refuse to believe. The chief priests and Pharisees, for example, were exasperated by Jesus' miracle. "From that day on they planned together to kill Him. . . . The chief priests planned to put Lazarus to death also" (John 11:53; 12:10). Read the rest of John 11 and through 12:11. Why do you think the Pharisees responded this way?

2. These were the people who were supposed to have been the closest to God! Yet they not only missed the point of God's

work, they were hostile to it. What can we, people who are supposed to be close to God, learn from them? What is the temptation that they—and we—face?

3. "Lazarus, come forth!" Four days dead, Lazarus returned to life, and grief was turned to joy, loss was turned to gain, emptiness was turned to fullness! "I am the resurrection and the life," Jesus tells us. And He showed us, not with fanfare and attention-grabbing drumroll, but with empathy, compassion, gentleness, and care. How has He been the resurrection and the life to you? How has He restored joy and fullness in your life?

4. As you join with each other under the Father's care, quietly and tenderly pray for those areas in one another's lives that need Jesus' life-giving words, the healing compassion of His tears. He won't scold or turn you away. He'll draw near to you, offering the comfort, grace, and hope you need.

Chapter 21

TRIUMPH FOR THE UNDESERVING

Selected Scripture

Tombstones are silent markers of lives passed, summaries of how loved ones feel about the now absent one or how that person felt about life. Some are profound, some tender, a few philosophical, and a handful even humorous—like this one from a cemetery in Massachusetts:

> Beneath this stone, a lump of clay
> Lies Arabella Young
> Who on the 21st of May
> Began to hold her tongue.[1]

Or try this one from a Georgia cemetery:

> "I told you I was sick!"[2]

In his immortal work on martyrs, John Fox exhumed remarks found on the burial markers of slain Christians. "Here lies Marcia, put to rest in a dream of peace," reads one, and "Victorious in peace and in Christ," reads another. Contrast their hope-filled messages with the despairing words on the graves of non-Christians, for example: "Live for the present hour, since we are sure of nothing else" and "Traveler, curse me not as you pass, for I am in darkness and cannot answer."[3]

Christian or not, hope-filled or despairing, all humans share the inevitability of death. But once death comes, our paths divide.

This chapter has been adapted from "Christ Is Raised, but What about Me?" from the Bible study guide *Questions Christians Ask*, written by David Lien, from the Bible-teaching ministry of Charles R. Swindoll (Fullerton, Calif.: Charles R. Swindoll, Inc., 1989).

1. Gyles Brandreth, *Famous Last Words and Tombstone Humor* (New York, N.Y.: Sterling Publishing Co., 1989), p. 82.

2. David Wallechinsky and Irving Wallace, *The People's Almanac* (Garden City, N.Y.: Doubleday and Co., 1975), p. 1320.

3. John Fox, *Fox's Book of Martyrs*, ed. William Byron Forbush (New York, N.Y.: Holt, Rinehart and Winston, n.d.), pp. 11–12.

The Dividing Line of Hope

Since the beginning of time, death has been a mystery. Even Job asked the question, "If a man dies, will he live again?" (Job 14:14). Though Job knew his ultimate destiny remained safely part of the sovereign plan of God, he still had questions. And so do we.

Death shakes all of us when it comes. As we discovered in the last chapter, Martha and Mary—and even Jesus—grieved over Lazarus' death. And though Martha believed in a future resurrection, the finality of her brother's death overwhelmed her.

Jesus' words to Martha, "I am the resurrection and the life (John 11:25)," bring hope to all believers when facing death—a hope nonbelievers can never know. Joseph Bayly, in his book *The Last Thing We Talk About*, tells a personal story that illustrates the dividing line between hope and desolation. Waiting to thank the doctor who had showed such compassion to his dying son, Bayly tried to offer hope to a grief-stricken mother whose young son was going through the same illness:

> "It's good to know, isn't it?" I spoke slowly, choosing my words with unusual care, "that even though the medical outlook is hopeless, we can have hope for our children in such a situation. We can be sure that after our child dies, he'll be completely removed from sickness and suffering and everything like that, and be completely well and happy."
>
> "If I could only believe that," the woman replied. "But I don't. When he dies, I'll just have to cover him up with dirt and forget I ever had him."[4]

So many people facing tragic circumstances walk through those times with no sense of hope beyond the grave. That is a horrible way to live. But an even more horrible way to die. Thankfully, Christ made another way to face both life *and* death with hope.

The Hope of Christ's Resurrection

Our hope for today and for our life beyond the grave is tied to the fact of Christ's resurrection. Because Jesus rose from the dead, we, too, will be raised as He was raised (see Rom. 6:3–11). To deny

4. Joseph Bayly, *The Last Thing We Talk About* (Elgin, Ill.: David C. Cook Publishing Co., 1969) p. 13.

our own hope of resurrection is to flatly deny Christ's resurrection. That's the point Paul emphasized when he wrote 1 Corinthians 15:

> If there is no resurrection of the dead, not even Christ has been raised; and if Christ has not been raised, then our preaching is vain, your faith also is vain. Moreover we are even found to be false witnesses of God, because we testified against God that He raised Christ, whom He did not raise, if in fact the dead are not raised. For if the dead are not raised, not even Christ has been raised; and if Christ has not been raised, your faith is worthless; you are still in your sins. Then those also who have fallen asleep in Christ have perished. If we have hoped in Christ in this life only, we are of all men most to be pitied. (vv. 13–19)

Paul made it abundantly clear that Christ's resurrection guarantees the same resurrection for all who believe in His name. Without the Resurrection, our faith is in vain, worthless, and our preaching of Christ just empty rhetoric. Without the Resurrection, Christ and all His promises would have decayed in the tomb. And without the hope of resurrection, we are *still in our sins*, spiritually dead, with no hope beyond death's door . . . a pitiful, hopeless lot.

Let's take a closer look at each fact of the Resurrection that Paul described in this passage. Together they will buttress our faith and reinforce our hope for today and our eternal tomorrow.

Since Christ Was Raised, Christians Will Rise

> But now Christ has been raised from the dead, the first fruits of those who are asleep. For since by a man came death, by a man also came the resurrection of the dead. For as in Adam all die, so also in Christ all will be made alive. But each in his own order: Christ the first fruits, after that those who are Christ's at His coming. (1 Cor. 15:20–23)

We simply cannot deny the connection between the fact of Christ's resurrection and the assurance of believers in Him. As Harold Mare explains:

> Certainly, Paul implies, none of the Corinthian believers would deny that an integral part of the

gospel message is the resurrection of Christ. Therefore, they must now accept the sequel—Christ guarantees the resurrection of the dead, as the word "firstfruits" teaches. By "firstfruits" Paul brings to bear the rich imagery of the OT. The "firstfruits"— the first sheaf of the harvest offered to the Lord (Lev. 23:10–11, 12, 20)—was not only prior to the main harvest but was also an assurance that the rest of the harvest was coming. . . . [Jesus] preceded his people in bodily resurrection and he is also the guarantee of their resurrection at his second coming.[5]

Since We Will Enter an Imperishable Heaven, We Will Need an Imperishable Body

Before we enter our eternal, imperishable dwelling place, our mortal bodies will be raised and changed. Later in the same chapter Paul wrote:

Behold, I tell you a mystery; we will not all sleep, but we will all be changed, in a moment, in the twinkling of an eye, at the last trumpet; for the trumpet will sound, and the dead will be raised imperishable, and we will be changed. For this perishable must put on the imperishable, and this mortal must put on immortality. (1 Cor. 15:51–53; see also vv. 39–49)

Commentator Bruce Winter explains that "for the Christian there is a guaranteed continuity of existence with the resurrection of his or her body and its transformation into the very likeness of Christ (compare Phil. 3:21)."[6] As John explains in his first letter:

Beloved, now we are children of God, and it has not appeared as yet what we will be. We know that when [Jesus] appears, we will be like Him, because we will see Him just as He is. (1 John 3:2)

5. W. Harold Mare, "1 Corinthians," in *The Expositor's Bible Commentary,* ed. Frank E. Gaebelein (Grand Rapids, Mich.: Zondervan Publishing House, 1976), vol. 10, p. 285.

6. Bruce Winter, "1 Corinthians," in *New Bible Commentary: 21st Century Edition,* 4th ed., rev. ed., ed. D. A. Carson and others (1994; reprint, Downers Grove, Ill.: InterVarsity Press, 2000), p. 1185.

The resurrection on the last day will be like going to a grand heavenly reunion! We'll be surrounded by people who will no longer cry, who no longer get sick, who never die, and who'll spend eternity with us in the presence of Jesus, the Lamb of God who took away the sins of the world.[7] Imagine the joy of it!

You Can Be Resurrected Too!

The promise of resurrection is for all who call on the name of Jesus by faith. S. Lewis Johnson, longtime pastor of Believers Chapel in Dallas, used to say, "The Resurrection is God's 'Amen' to Christ's statement, 'It is finished.'" And our resurrection will be God's final "Amen" to the words we prayed when we trusted in Christ as our Savior. That hope is not just for the future, but it is a genuine source of strength for the struggles we face today.

Hope of Resurrection Brings Strength for Life's Heartaches

Live long enough and the waves of tragic circumstances will soon pound against the peaceful shores of your life. They often roll in with news of the sudden death of a loved one. Or when you hear the word *cancer*. You've probably already experienced such times. Though we may initially feel despair, as believers we can know peace and even joy amidst those stormy gales. How? Because of the hope of the resurrection. We know that pain, confusion, fear, and death don't have the final say—life, healing, comfort, and reunion do. Death can never steal hope's power. That hope rests firmly on the truths that flow from these words:

> But when this perishable will have put on the im-
> perishable, and this mortal will have put on immor-
> tality, then will come about the saying that is
> written, "Death is swallowed up in victory. O death,
> where is your victory? O death, where is your sting?"
> The sting of death is sin, and the power of sin is the
> law; but thanks be to God, who gives us the victory
> through our Lord Jesus Christ. (1 Cor. 15:54–57)

That's not Shakespeare. That's the apostle Paul exclaiming the joyous hope Christians have beyond the grave. And his words are the greatest epitaph of all!

---

7. Adapted from Charles R. Swindoll, *The Darkness and the Dawn: Empowered by the Tragedy and Triumph of the Cross* (Nashville, Tenn.: Word Publishing, 2001), pp. 310–11.

A Final Thought

In the shadow of the cemetery, when death's darkness threatens to overwhelm us with fear, there is one bright hope: the hope of resurrection.

Do you know the Source of that hope? Has His shining light warmed you in the cold hours of your darkest nights? Jesus is there for you, dispelling the darkness and pointing you toward a new day yet to dawn. Just like the Son, you, too, will rise one day!

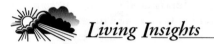 *Living Insights*

It's difficult for us to imagine what the disciples experienced as they watched their Master die on the cross that day. Especially Peter. He left *everything* to follow Jesus. Peter's excitement of being part of Christ's triumphant new kingdom waned quickly, however, as Jesus bowed His head in death.

Most of us have felt our hope ebb at times, as well. In those times of disillusionment, loneliness, and pain, we need a message of hope. Yet it's possible that we've never really stopped to consider our basis for hope as Christians and how that hope can enrich our lives.

You're invited to do that sort of reflection now. Before each of the following questions, a quote is provided to help spark your thinking. Take a moment to ponder the quotes before writing your responses.

> Loneliness.
> It's a cry. A moan, a wail. It's a gasp whose origin is the recesses of our souls.
> Can you hear it? The abandoned child. The divorcée. The quiet home. The empty mailbox. The long days. The longer nights. A one-night stand. A forgotten birthday. A silent phone.[8]

Loneliness most always accompanies the death of someone you love. There's no escaping that relentless emotion. How can the hope you have in Christ help you cope with it? What conditions

---

8. Max Lucado, *No Wonder They Call Him the Savior* (Portland, Ore.: Multnomah Press, 1986), p. 45.

do you tend to place on the Lord before you'll trust Him with your loneliness?

_____

_____

_____

_____

_____

_____

_____

The most gut-wrenching cry of loneliness in history came not from a prisoner or a widow or a patient. It came from a hill, from a cross, from a Messiah.

"My God, my God!" he screamed, "Why did you abandon me!"

Never have words carried so much hurt. Never has one being been so lonely.[9]

How does the pain of your own suffering deepen your relationship with Christ? In what ways does knowing the depth of His loneliness and pain comfort you in your hours of intense grief and loss?

_____

_____

_____

_____

_____

_____

_____

9. Lucado, *No Wonder They Call Him the Savior*, p. 47.

How can your hope of future resurrection lift you out of despair today?

_____

_____

_____

_____

_____

_____

_____

_____

> Blessed be the God and Father of our Lord Jesus Christ, who according to His great mercy has caused us to be born again to a living hope through the resurrection of Jesus Christ from the dead.

What's this? Another quote to think about for a moment and pass by? No. The apostle Peter wrote that in 1 Peter 1:3. Will you make his words your own today?

 Questions for Group Reflection

Because Jesus lives, we live! He has not only gone before us into death, to atone for our sins and reconcile us to God, but He has also burst forth from the grave to lead us into life. As Paul wrote to the Colossians, "He rescued us from the domain of darkness, and transferred us to the kingdom of His beloved Son" (1:13).

1. What kind of new life does Jesus lead us into? How does our new life differ from the darkness of the world around us?

2. How does Jesus's resurrection reveal God's love and its power? How is His love a force of new life in your life?

New Testament scholar N. T. Wright illuminates a further meaning of Jesus' resurrection:

> Easter is all about the wiping away of tears. . . .
>
> . . . Without Easter, there is no reason to suppose that good will triumph over evil, that love will win over hatred, that life will win over death. But with Easter we have hope; because hope depends on love; and love has become human and has died, and is now alive for evermore, and holds the keys of Death and Hades. It is because of him that we know—we don't just hope, we *know*—that God will wipe away all tears from all eyes. . . . In that knowledge we find that the hand that dries *our* tears passes the cloth on to us, and bids us follow him, to go to dry one another's tears.[10]

3. As you come together in prayer, bring your tears to the Lord as a child brings a hurt to a gentle parent. Then bring the hurts of others you know to the Lord, and ask Him to show you how you can help wipe their tears away.

10. N. T. Wright, *Following Jesus: Biblical Reflections on Discipleship* (Grand Rapids, Mich.: William B. Eerdmans Publishing Co., 1995), pp. 58, 61–62.

Chapter 22

HOPE FOR THE UNFORGIVEN
1 Corinthians 15:12–19

What's the big deal about Easter? Why all the hubbub about some prophet of old who supposedly was raised from the dead? That is certainly hard to believe . . . and even harder to prove. So why make such a fuss year after year about an event that may or may not have even occurred? Why not just settle for a celebration of springtime, with tulips and eggs and pastel-colored baskets and bonnets? Seems more rational and a lot less fanciful.

Why Easter? That was the question the apostle Paul answered directly when he wrote his letter to the Corinthian believers twenty centuries ago. Only, his answer had nothing to do with bunnies and eggs and bonnets and baskets. His answer carried a much more serious tone.

The Question of the Ages

> But if there is no resurrection of the dead, not even Christ has been raised; and if Christ has not been raised, then our preaching is vain, your faith also is vain. Moreover we are even found to be false witnesses of God, because we witnessed against God that He raised Christ, whom He did not raise, if in fact the dead are not raised. For if the dead are not raised, not even Christ has been raised; and if Christ has not been raised, your faith is worthless; you are still in your sins. (1 Cor. 15:13–17)

Without the Resurrection, life would be pretty bleak. Especially for the Christian. Paul says that without the hope of resurrection, Christ has not been raised . . . there is no hope, our preaching is vain, our witnessing is false, our faith is worthless and our forgiveness is only a dream. Suddenly we're back where we started—a people sitting in darkness, hopelessly lost in our sins. That's a lot more serious than bunnies and bonnets, don't you agree?

Can you imagine what your life would be like without *forgiveness*? Hollywood did. They gathered together a group of movie producers and film stars and, under the direction of Clint Eastwood, produced the 1992 blockbuster film *Unforgiven.*

Here's the basic plot: Clint Eastwood played the main character —a gunslinger who returns to the life he had left and one by one kills all the bad guys in town. After that he returns to his now dilapidated farm and to his unhappy children, whom he finds standing by the grave of his dead wife. After some strange, dark dialogue, the picture goes black and the credits roll.

Great way to end a movie, huh? Bleakness, unhappiness, despair, and sorrow. No happy reunion, no tearful reconciliation in the arms of a grateful family. None of that. Only a final scene of death, sadness, and hopelessness. A grim picture of life without forgiveness.

In the words of Chuck Swindoll:

> If you have been in the Christian life so long that you've forgotten what life is like without hope, you need a good dose of the message in that film. It is as pointless, meaningless, empty, and torturous as you can imagine, and then some. Anger, ugliness, and sadness prevail. Then there's the grave scene at the end, and the credits roll. There's no joy, no relief, no rewards—no hope![1]

Let's Pretend . . .

Let's spend some time laying our own script for a movie that depicts life without forgiveness. We'll base it on four main characters and their lives. Our director will be none other than—you guessed it—Clint Easterless!

UNFORGIVEN: ACT I

Scene 1: The first man is Little Joe, the youngest in a large family, and his older brothers hate him because he's the favored son. Daddy loves Little Joe so much that he buys him a special coat. He never buys the other boys anything. The older brothers resent Little Joe, and their resentment soon turns to hatred.

One day the brothers go on an overnight campout. While they are away from home, one of the

---

1. Charles R. Swindoll, *The Darkness and the Dawn: Empowered by the Tragedy and Triumph of the Cross* (Nashville: Word Publishing, 2001), p. 325.

brothers says, "Now's the time to get rid of Little Joe." So they tie him up and drop him in a pit.

"Let's let him die there," they say. "The animals will eat him. Good riddance."

So they take Little Joe's coat, smear it with the blood of a wolf they've killed, and then they plot to tell their daddy that Little Joe was killed by a vicious wild animal.

Then one of the boys gets a better idea. Spotting a camel caravan in the distance, he says, "Why should we leave him to die? Let's sell him and make some money." So they hail the caravan, which is on its way to Egypt, and they sell their brother into slavery for twenty bucks.

As the scene fades out, Little Joe is watching his brothers walk away laughing, counting their money.

Scene 2: In the land of Egypt, Little Joe is nothing more than chattel—a piece of flesh to be bought and sold. He becomes a slave in the household of a government official, and there he becomes a favorite of the owner of the house. Unfortunately, he also becomes the favorite of the wife of the owner of the house. Little Joe is tall, dark, and handsome, and she wants him. But she stands against everything he stands for, and he resists her advances.

Angered by his rejection, the wicked mistress of the household gets her revenge by crying "Rape!" Her husband believes her and throws Little Joe in jail, leaving him imprisoned there for years for a crime he didn't commit.

Eventually, through an interesting chain of events, the king of the land hears that Little Joe can interpret dreams. The king has an audience with Little Joe, who tells him the future of the land of Egypt. Almost overnight Little Joe is promoted to a place of authority and soon becomes prime minister.

Scene 3: Meanwhile, back on the ranch, Little Joe's brothers are raising their families and doing well, despite the fact that their father has never stopped mourning for the youngest son he believes is dead.

Then a recession hits. The brothers lose their jobs. Word reaches them that someone in Egypt has a storehouse of food and that he is willing to provide a handout to those who are homeless or needy. The brothers make their way to Egypt, not knowing that they will be asking help from their long-lost brother.

This is a great moment in the film, and director Clint Easterless makes the most of it. The brothers don't know who the prime minister is, but he recognizes them. He has them imprisoned and tortured, then condemns them all to terrible deaths.

Unforgiven: Act II

Scene 1: The next scene introduces us to a character named Sammy. His parents are devout people, and God tells them, through the words of an angel, that their son will be special to God. Not only will he become judge—the most prominent position among their people—but he will be a powerful force to slay the enemies of their people and Almighty God. He will be the mightiest and strongest man in the land. He won't have to lift weights or train at a local fitness center. He will be strong because God will make him strong.

The secret of Sammy's strength lies in the special vows that he must take. Mainly, he must never cut his hair. Furthermore, he must never imbibe in strong drink. He must be careful about what he eats and steer clear of dead carcasses.

Scene 2: When Sammy becomes a man, however, his private battle with lust begins to control him. He does become a judge, but he also falls in love with a girl named Lila, from among the enemy of his people. He becomes more intimate with Lila than he had ever been with his own God and he tells her the secret of his life. With his head in her lap, he mumbles, "My strength is in my hair." Then he falls asleep. Because he has entered the city of the enemy, he is an easy target. They cut off his hair, down to the scalp.

When Sammy awakens, he's bald as an egg and has no strength. Worse than that, he has no God.

His enemies blind him, and he spends the rest of his days as a grinder in the prison house, walking mindlessly around and around, pushing the huge wheel that grinds the grain.

Easterless concludes the scene with a final shot of despair, showing Sammy slumped on his knees, face-down in the mud and manure as he breathes his last —a blind man caught in the tentacles of his own lust.

Unforgiven: Act III

Scene 1: The final act opens with a bang as the lens focuses on the third character, a young "rebel without a cause." We first see him when he tells his father, "I'm through with this family. I don't want to spend another night under this roof. Just give me what I've got coming, and I'm out of here."

His father writes him a check, and the boy slams the door behind him.

Scene 2: The teenager is riding high—from Reno to Vegas he's on a roll. He skis through Colorado and roars on to Chicago and New York. He's got a whole gang of fast friends who want to be with him, because he's the boy with the bucks. He can get whatever he wants: drugs, booze, women—lots of women.

But suddenly he runs out of bucks. And when you're out of bucks, you're out of buddies. His friends pull out. The women walk away. He can't even win the lottery.

He rides the rails back across the country. When he gets to Iowa, he gets off and takes a walk down a country road. He meets a pig farmer, and before nightfall he's knee-deep in swine slop. At night he slumps into a cold dirty bunk—that night and the next night and the next, until he realizes that every single thing he wants is really back home with his dad.

Early the next morning, he washes himself off as best he can and hitchhikes the rest of the way home.

Scene 3: But in an Easterless film, you can't go home

again. When his father answers the door, he says bitterly, "What do you want?"

"I . . . I'm . . . I'm back," says the thin-and-dirty kid.

"You're back? There's no place for you here. Listen, you got what you wanted, now live with it. Look at what you've done with yourself! You're a miserable wreck. You stink. Get out of my life!" The door slams, and the boy has nowhere to go but down.

The final scene shows the boy sitting in a seedy room on Skid Row, holding a pistol to his head. As the scene fades, there's a gunshot. And the credits roll.[2]

Why Easter Matters

Without the Resurrection there would be no Easter. No forgivenss of sins. No hope of mercy and grace. No new beginnings for lives gone wrong. Grudges reign. Revenge rules. That's life without the hope of resurrection . . . without forgiveness.

Thankfully, that's not the way God intends for anyone to live. And that's why the stories on which our movie script was based have, in reality, very different endings.

Little Joe is Joseph from the book of Genesis (see chapters 37, 39–45). When he realized that it was his brothers who had come to him begging for food, his heart ached; he offered forgiveness and supplied them with the food they and their father needed to survive. What actually occurred was a grand, emotional family reunion! Joseph didn't take revenge. He could have, but he didn't. He didn't torture his brothers or condemn them to a cruel death. He could have, but he didn't. Joseph forgave his brothers because he understood that life is full of hope when there is the promise of resurrection.

Then there was Sammy. He's actually Samson from Judges 14–16. He did allow his foolish lusts to get the best of him. When his hair was cut, he lost his strength, his sight, and his integrity. Remarkably, his hair grew back as an amazing testimony to God's grace, mercy, and *forgiveness*. His strength restored and, more importantly, his relationship with the Lord renewed, he completed the mission God had originally called him to do. That's grace. That's forgiveness. That's a happy ending!

2. Swindoll, *The Darkness and the Dawn: Empowered by the Tragedy and Triumph of the Cross*, pp. 325–329.

The last story in our script was based on, of course, the parable of the prodigal son. In the biblical version of the story, the father didn't angrily slam the door in his son's face when he returned home with hat in hand, rather, he ran to meet him. He threw a party for him and reinstituted him into the family. Nothing had been lost. In fact, their relationship was strengthened by the son's brokenness and the father's compassionate forgiveness. What had once been lost had now been found!

That is the message of resurrection . . . death no longer reigns over us! We have been set free form the penalty of death by Christ's triumphant resurrection. We are no longer in our sins if we've called upon His name alone, by faith alone.

Thanks be to God . . . He is risen . . . He is risen indeed!

 Living Insights

In Paul's day a motto that hung in Athens read, "Once a man dies and the earth drinks up his blood, there is no resurrection." Paul hotly disagreed. Now, some may say, "Well, when Athens died, so died the doubt of resurrection." Are you kidding? As recently as the nineteenth century there was a poem spreading around England that has caught all kinds of people off guard. Charles Swinburne wrote it.

> From too much love of living,
> From hope and fear set free,
> We thank with brief thanksgiving
> Whatever gods may be
> That no life lives forever;
> That dead men rise up never;
> That even the weariest river
> Winds somewhere safe to sea.

It's a lie! Dead men rise up *ever*! And there is no safety at sea apart from Christ! The resurrection is our only hope.[3]

Is it yours today?

3. Charles R. Swindoll, *The Tale of the Tardy Oxcart and 1,501 Other Stories* (Nashville: Word Publishing, 1998), p. 492.

BOOKS FOR
PROBING FURTHER

We have reached the end of our long journey from the darkness to the dawn. And what a glorious journey it has been! We pray that you have discovered some important truths about the person, character, and work of Jesus Christ through your study. We also hope that this book has helped you gain a more profound understanding of the events surrounding His passion and resurrection.

To provide you with the opportunity to explore these topics more deeply, we wish to recommend the following books. As you continue your travels through the Christian life, we hope these books will make the road more smooth and the journey more refreshing.

Bishop, Jim. *The Day Christ Died*. San Francisco, Calif.: Harper Books, 1991.

Bonhoeffer, Dietrich. *Meditations on the Cross*. Louisville, Ky.: Westminster John Knox Press, 1998.

Brown, Raymond E. *The Death of the Messiah from Gethsemane to the Grave: A Commentary on the Passion Narratives in the Four Gospels*. Volumes 1–2. New York, N.Y.: Doubleday Books, 1994.

Fischer, John. *On a Hill Too Far Away: Putting the Cross Back into the Center of Our Lives*. Minneapolis, Minn.: Bethany House Publishers, 2001.

Johnson, Luke Timothy. *Living Jesus: Learning the Heart of the Gospel*. San Francisco, Calif.: Harper Books, 2000.

Kiehl, Erich H. *The Passion of Our Lord*. Grand Rapids, Mich.: Baker Book House Company, 1990.

Lightner, Robert P. *The Death Christ Died: A Biblical Case for Unlimited Atonement*. Grand Rapids, Mich.: Kregel Publications, 1998.

Lloyd-Jones, Martyn. *The Cross*. Westchester, Ill.: Crossway Books, 1986.

Lucado, Max. *The Cross: Selected Writings and Images*. Sisters, Ore.: Multnomah Publishers Inc., 1998.

———. *He Chose the Nails.* Nashville, Tenn.: Word Publishing, 2000.

———. *Six Hours One Friday: Anchoring to the Power of the Cross.* New York, N.Y.: Walker & Co., 1996.

———. *And the Angels Were Silent: The Final Week of Jesus.* Sisters, Ore.: Multnomah Publishers Inc., 1999.

Mattison, Judith. *The Seven Last Words of Christ: The Message of the Cross for Today.* Minneapolis, Minn.: Augsburg Fortress Press, 1992.

Neuhaus, Richard John. *Death on a Friday Afternoon: Meditations on the Last Words of Jesus From the Cross.* New York, N.Y.: Basic Books, 2000.

Stott, John. *The Cross of Christ.* Downers Grove, Ill.: InterVarsity Press, 1986.

Strobel, Lee. *The Case for Christ: A Journalist's Personal Investigation of the Evidence for Jesus.* Grand Rapids, Mich.: Zondervan Publishing House, 1998.

Swindoll, Charles. *The Darkness and the Dawn: Empowered by the Tragedy and Triumph of the Cross.* Nashville, Tenn.: Word Publishing, 2001.

Some of the books listed may be out of print and available only through a library. For those currently available, please contact your local Christian bookstore. Books by Charles R. Swindoll may be obtained through the Insight for Living Resource Center, as well as many books by other authors. Just call the IFL office that serves you.

Insight for Living also has Bible study guides available on many books of the Bible as well as on a variety of topics, Bible characters, and contemporary issues. For more information, see the ordering instructions that follow and contact the office that serves you.

NOTES

NOTES

NOTES

NOTES

NOTES

NOTES

NOTES

NOTES

Ordering Information

The Darkness and the Dawn

If you would like to order additional Bible study guides, purchase the audiocassette series that accompanies this guide, or request our product catalogs, please contact the office that serves you.

United States and International locations:

Insight for Living
Post Office Box 269000
Plano, TX 75026-9000

1-800-772-8888, 24 hours a day, seven days a week (U.S. contacts) International constituents may contact the U.S. office through mail queries.

Canada:

Insight for Living Ministries
Post Office Box 2510
Vancouver, BC, Canada V6B 3W7

1-800-663-7639, 24 hours a day, seven days a week
InfoCanada@insight.org

Australia:

Insight for Living, Inc.
20 Albert Street
Blackburn, VIC 3130, Australia

Toll-free 1800 772 888 or (03) 9877-4277, 8:30 A.M. to 5:00 P.M., Monday to Friday
iflaus@insight.org

Internet:

www.insight.org

Bible Study Guide Subscription Program

Bible study guide subscriptions are available. Please call or write the office nearest you to find out how you can receive our Bible study guides on a regular basis.